John Foley
40 Sylvester Hamilton Rd.
Chester, MA 01011

MY SEARCH FOR TRACES OF GOD

MY SEARCH FOR TRACES OF GOD

by Philip S. Callahan, Ph.D.

Copyright © 1997 by Philip S. Callahan

Acres U.S.A.
P.O. Box 8800, Metairie, Louisiana 70011

Callahan, Philip S., 1923-
 Traces of God: miracles in my life / by Philip S. Callahan. —
Metairie, La. : Acres U.S.A., 1997
 p. cm.
 Includes index.
 ISBN 0-911311-54-8

 1. Religious Philosophy.   2. Miracles.   3. Paramagnetism.   I.
Title.

Library of Congress Catalog Card Number: 97-071970

ABOUT THE COVER

Pictured is the center portion of a beautiful fresco on the walls of the convent chapel on top of Tepeyac Hill in Mexico City. It shows a magpie, which is not found in Mexico, defending the Virgin Mary from Juan Diego. The Virgin stands on a rock, not on an angel as depicted in the real image. The angel, dress decorations, and sunburst have been added in this fresco to the original, simple, inexplicable image.

DEDICATION

I dedicate this book with love to the five mothers in my life:

The Blessed Virgin Mary, mother of Jesus Christ.
Winnie, mother of our four children.
Enid Ainsa Callahan, my own mother — in heaven.
Ann Theresa Harris, my sister — mother of three.
Doreen Callahan, mother of seven, my sister-in-law —
in heaven.

CONTENTS

THE PAINTING

God reveals Himself to the humble in the lowliest of disguises, but the proud, who never look below the surface, fail to find Him even in His greatest manifestations.

Abandonment to Divine Providence
Jean-Pierre De Caussade

My frontispiece shows the five-inch (life-size) male English or house sparrow, *Passer domesticus*, searching for aphids on the beautiful purple flower head of the wavy-leaf thistle, *Cirsium undulatum*, a common thistle in Kansas.

At Kansas State University in Manhattan, Kansas, I often watched English sparrows clutching this thistle which grew wild in the poor soil of poisoned, chemically farmed, Kansas fields.

The male English sparrow is distinguished from the real sparrow family (it is a weaver bird) by the robust body, very slightly forked tail, and large head and beak. It is the only "sparrow" with a large black bib under its chin.

Although the active little bird feeds on seed, it is mainly a ground feeder, so most seed is waste from harvest practices.

Unlike red-winged blackbirds, which will destroy corn ears while searching for corn earworm larvae at the silken corn tip, the sparrow feeds mainly on insects from open plant heads. The sparrow frequents five or six different thistle species looking not for flower seeds but aphids hidden away among the bristles of the spiny leafed plants — in short, it is a beneficial "sparrow."

FOREWORD

Some few years ago, Barry Commoner used his book, *The Closing Circle: Nature, Man, and Technology*, to describe how everything was related to everything else. His quest was an understanding of ecology that required a new assessment of the paradigm under which academia labored. The idea that the world was an integrated whole had been around since the time of Socrates, but this idea retained its foothold only in the minds of mystics like the Indian Chief Seattle — and the likes of Phil Callahan. Descartes and Newton and all the reductionists in effect detoured the human spirit from its natural goal — namely integration of the web of life.

During his post-World War II walk around the world, Callahan refined his thinking on the cyclical processes of nature. The experiments that led to his classic *Tuning in to Nature* gave way, soon enough, to see the phenomenon of life not as isolated objects, but as a veritable network of living systems — interconnected and interdependent. At a time when most scientists saw insects and microbial populations as life forms infected by a demonology, Callahan saw the value of all life forms, with *Homo sapiens* only one of God's noble creatures. The spiritual and religious connection has never escaped Callahan. His expressions to this effect inserted power and majesty into his hauntingly beautiful little book, *The Soul of the Ghost Moth.*

But those who want to commune with the real soul of Phil Callahan will best confer their meditation on the pages of this volume. Although a first-rate scientist who usually instructs and often baffles his colleagues, Callahan is at his best when he annihilates the reductionist model by explaining the idea of belonging and connectedness to the cosmos as a whole. He gently drives home the point that eco-farming is spiritual in its deepest essence.

The mix of biographical vignettes with profound scientific truths and religious experiences make this scientific-social-religious philosopher a unique man for our time. Someone once wrote of Callahan, "He is a 2,000-year-old man who finds himself at home with scientific apparatus and computerization, never once forgetting that man really can't synthesize anything, if the term is taken to mean making a copy of the Creator's handiwork."

It takes a high degree of literacy to comprehend the essence of this Callahan volume, and yet those who follow his work will find each personal experience in this book laced together with a scientific truth as pure as the sound of a glass bell.

When Phil Callahan first explained how insects communicate with each other and with plants, he proposed more than a challenge to the failed eco-ethical standards of that hour. In the same careful way that William A. Albrecht described scientists who asked the wrong question, Callahan called on the carpet colleagues who pursued life-destroying adventures and goals. Without mentioning the crimes or their perpetrators, Callahan in effect chided physicists who spend their God-given talents building new weapons systems, chemists who contaminate the beautiful planet on which we live, and biologists who tamper with and release life forms with little or no understanding of what their microorganisms will do.

Callahan's eco-ethics have their formulations in the lives of saints and holy places possessed of paramagnetism, in his observations of nature's wonders, and in the microbial workers that keep mankind and animals from crashing into extinction.

Go to page one, then follow the trail of life as lived by ecology's favored science philosopher. The reward should be weighed out on a jeweler's scale, it is that precious.

— *Charles Walters*

P.S. Callahan

waves of time

in deep forest shade
inch worms inch

in deep forest shade
cuckoos coo

in deep forest shade
the rain bird
stalks
the crawl of time
which
in deep forest shade

is neither
then
nor
now

in deep forest shade
inch worms, inch
and escape
now
and again
across
God's
frame of time

Relativity

PROLOGUE

Mules, Weeds and Sparrows

*What I tell you in darkness, that speak ye in light: and
what ye hear in the ear, that preach ye upon the housetops.
And fear not them which will kill the body, but are not
able to kill the soul: but rather fear him which is able to
destroy both soul and body in hell.* ·
*Are not two sparrows sold for a farthing? And one of them
shall not fall on the ground without the father.
But the very hairs on your head are all numbered.
Fear ye not therefore, ye are of more value than many
sparrows.*

Matthew 10:27-31

I have a favorite plant — it is the common thistle. I also
have a favorite bird — it is the English (or house) sparrow.
The first is a weed cursed by farmers, the second a bird
damned by bird lovers and city folk alike. One might say that
they are both misfits of society and considered quite detri-
mental to man's technical empire. Like the noble mule, they
are much maligned.

Throughout my life I have had considerable experience
with weeds, sparrows, and, though city bred, with mules. The
mule, which should be admired because it built America, is

considered stubborn and mean but, in fact, is smart and lovable. The mule is considered stubborn by those who have never worked with the animal, which includes most modern Americans. Moderns are hardly qualified to judge mules. They little understand that the history of America rests on the strong backs of mules. Mules pulled over half the covered wagons westward, packed or freighted goods, worked deep in mines and backed the famed all black 24th and 25th infantries in the Indian wars.

My daughter, six- and eight-year-old grandsons, and I once took a mule named Blackjack across the High Sierras where there was no trail. It was on this journey that I learned that, like me, mules love thistles. My love is aesthetic, Blackjack's love was his stomach. He considered the common sow thistle a real delicacy. He would pull back his upper lip and devour the thistle, flower spines and all, in few delicate bites. Blackjack was of course nipping at the Sierra thistle (*Cirsium californicum*) and not the common, or hog, thistle (*Cirsium vulgar*).

Blackjack, our companion mule, was most certainly not stubborn. What the misguided call stubborn we found to be mule common sense. Blackjack would not do anything that, in his humble opinion, might lead to serious injury.

The ancient Hebrews considered the mule to be a forbidden animal. The crossbred mule was an "impure" hybrid between a horse and a donkey. In that belief there was a considerable amount of hypocrisy for whenever it was necessary to get from one point to another across the rocky terrain of ancient Palestine, the mule was first choice. In fact, the Hebrew kings always rode mules. In *Kings I* we read:

The king also said unto them, take with you the servant of your Lord, and cause Solomon my son to ride upon my own mule, and bring him down to Gihon.

Obviously King David did not trust his son to a camel or donkey.

In *Esther* we find that the messengers that saved Esther's people were couriers sent out on muleback from King Ahasuerus:

So the posts that rode upon mules and camels went out being hastened and pressed on by the King's commandments.

Camels were fine for flat desert, but across dangerous, rocky, mountainous terrain only mules would suffice.

I call the mule noble for in biblical times kings always rode a mule. Christ as "King of the Jews" probably rode a mule and not a donkey into Jerusalem. We may also be certain that Christ loved weeds and sparrows, as he used them on numerous occasions in his parables (see *Matthew 10:27-31*, presented as a heading to this chapter).

Weeds, especially the thistle, have been condemned since man first discovered high-tech agriculture. Notice I say high-tech, for in earlier days fields were left fallow to weeds in alternate years. The weeds were then cut and sandwiched between cow and mule manure to fertilize the crops.

In olden days, farmers recognized that excessive thistle growth meant depleted soil — in short, thistles told the farmer that he did something wrong. Like the disappearance of the peregrine falcon warning us of DDT in the environment, thistles warn the farmer of dead, useless soil. Thistles grow where crops will not. That is precisely why their tender leaves make delicious survival food beside over-compacted — dead soil —

hiking trails. My love of thistles is both survival oriented (for food) and aesthetically oriented. Thistles are indeed beautiful plants just as English sparrows are beautiful birds.

I am not sure where my love of house sparrows originated except that my earliest love of birds centered on this fiesty little city creature. Among the old apartment houses of Memphis, where I spent my childhood, it was the only bird to "bird watch." As an unrelenting bird watcher, I not only observed house sparrows but trapped a few for pets. To my sorrow they invariably died — I have since learned to stick to watching birds.

A review of sparrow literature shows that this marvelous little bird has been stigmatized with almost every name in the book: pernicious, disreputable, quarrelsome and, worst of all, injurious. I have never been sure what this species injured, as the ones I observed lived mostly on weed seeds and scavengered in parking lots and open spaces for bits of cast-off human food.

They are most certainly not ugly birds. In fact, the male with his rust-colored back, black bib, and white cheeks is indeed one of the prettier of the sparrow group. The fact is, the species is not a sparrow at all, but in the weaver finch family that had its origin in Africa and the Middle East. It was most certainly the "sparrow" that Christ knew so well as it was among the most common birds in Palestine. The famous Massachusetts naturalist, Edward Howe Forbush, in his book of essays on the *Natural History of Birds*, writes that it is the "sparrow" mentioned in the Bible and other ancient literatures.

While I love English sparrows because of fond boyhood memories, I cannot logically give a reason why I have always had a longing for birds in general. Of course, neither can the other six million bird watchers in the United States. Six million is a rather large figure given by that wonderful organization the Audubon Society.

Likewise, I cannot understand why I am so devoted to the Virgin Mary. It probably also started in my early childhood when I received a beautiful creche for Christmas. That image of mother and child became glued in my memory.

Tradition has it that the Virgin Mary loved birds, and I like to imagine the house sparrow is the one she most often watched outside her kitchen door. Indeed my instinct, which is usually very reliable, leads me to believe that she fed bread crumbs to the little birds.

In ancient days, Middle-Eastern houses were partially devoid of furniture, and for that reason carpenters like St. Joseph and Jesus certainly spent most of their time fashioning wooden agricultural tools such as plows, yokes, camel saddles and mule saddles. Christ would have understood that mules, sparrows and weeds were considered nature's sinners. He thus utilized them to teach us about the evils of hypocrisy.

If there is one thing that we should learn from the New Testament it is that both Christ and his mother loved sinners — thieves, adulterers, and the like — very much, but detested hypocrisy. In all of his parables Christ seemed to be saying that the mules, weeds and sparrows of mankind can be forgiven, but there is little hope for the hypocrite. These are the people who, like Pharisees, point to their own importance and goodness while taking food from the mouths of the poor and humble.

This book is about the hypocrisy of the "pharisees" of modern high-tech. It is also about the life of scientists among the mules, sparrows and weeds of the world, of which I might add this author is one. There is today a high-tech hypocrisy in modern society that ignores God and destroys creation while pretending to be mankind's savior — population control by abortion, farming with chemical poisons, deadly drugs, and, of course, war with super bombs, nerve gas and lasers.

I sincerely believe that the numerous Marian apparitions that suddenly seem to be occurring all over the world are loving warnings of a mother to her children about the worship of that modern Satan, namely high technology. High-tech, it would seem, has degenerated into a high-profit enterprise based on greed and the human love of comfort at all cost.

This is also a book about the soil. The ultimate death of mankind begins with the death of living soil.

Most of my life has been spent as an agricultural scientist. My work began with a belief that high-tech, in the form of insecticides, could save us from the scourge of crop destruction by the hordes of insects so well described in the Bible. Slowly I came to realize that poisons only increase the worldwide problem of crop destruction by killing the soil.

If some of my fellow scientists would label me naive in my belief that God knows more of nature (His creation) than the scientists of high-tech corporations or universities, then that is their problem, not mine.

Others of a more loving nature might enjoy reading about God and mules. This is the story of one with a great love for Mary and her Son, and a firm belief that prayer, and not technology, will save our spaceship planet. Since I am a confirmed optimist, I have no doubt that the earth will be saved through the goodness of God — perhaps with a little help from mules, weeds and sparrows.

NOTE ON BLOCK CUTS

All of these block cuts were designed by cutting a figure, drawn on the block, with a sharp chisel, leaving a shallow groove (negative). The block was not inked (which leaves a black negative figure) but copied, with little difficulty, on a photocopy machine. This produces a positive image instead of a negative. Since the photocopy machine is a radiation mechanism, this is most certainly a non-photographic radiation figure produced from a negative.

Some Shroud of Turin researchers say this is not possible. Speaking of ancient times, I believe they are absolutely correct, but modern technology enables us to do many things, including fly, that the ancients could not accomplish.

There is nothing wrong with modern technology, only with what is called high-tech which, often as not, involves the amoral destruction of nature by clear cutting, habitat destruction for quick profit, chemical poisons, abortion, etc. Do not think that is an anti-technology book — I utilize technology, an example is seen in these block cuts.

PART I

Nature and War — A Background

God reveals Himself to us through the most commonplace happenings in a way just as mysterious and just as truly and as worthy of adoration as in the great occurrences of history and the scriptures.

Abandonment to Divine Providence
Jean-Pierre De Caussade

CHAPTER I
Outside the Kitchen Door

I see my way as birds their trackless way,
I shall arrive! what time, what circuit first,
I ask not: but unless God send His hail
Or blinding fireballs, sleet or stifling snow,
In some time, His good time, I shall arrive:
He guides me and the bird. In His good time!

Paracelsus, Part I
Elizabeth Barrett Browning

I am told by my sister Ann that I almost died a horrible death at birth, but that is a story for another time. Today, as I sit at my desk, I will write about my lesser love — nature.

God, my wife, and my children are my primary love. How can one such love be a multiple love? I confess I do not know except that God sent them my way. I do not understand why it is so, anymore than I can understand how God is multiple — a trinity. I do know that my earthly trinity has been God, family and nature, and that for good reasons God and family stand apart from nature.

Presumably, if our Christian heritage is a correct interpretation, God and family will be together for eternity while nature will perish in God's fireball. This is a paradox that, in my opinion, explains why man seeks to destroy nature for his own pleasure and comfort. This is perhaps why he seeks to justify that destruction by separating God's will, God's desire for life, from nature.

To modern science nature is as dead as God, or to use a metaphor, as dead as the little English sparrow I trapped outside my kitchen door.

I barely remember my early life in Memphis, Tennessee, but I have no such lukewarm memories of my later teenage years in Denver, Colorado. I do vaguely remember my sister being born in Memphis and my father bringing my brother and I a broken-beaked hummingbird. It had flown against our kitchen window and split its beak (1). He showed us how to feed it until it recovered. That seemed to be the beginning of the strange passion I have for nature and, in particular, birds — a passion otherwise unexplainable. I remember that at some time later, after we moved to Denver, I decided that what I needed to possess more than any earthly object was a bird book.

My father and mother were of the same mind, for one Christmas they put the red, blue, and green books of *Birds of America* in my stocking. Those were the days when a ten-cent store actually was a ten-cent store, and these small pocket-size books, with their stilted color plates, sold for a couple of dimes. These books became my indispensable field companions. They were narrow, barely three inches wide, and were thin enough to slide easily into my pants pockets. Their miniaturization was copied in World War II. What GI does not remember the Armed Services editions that he carried in his jacket pocket as he rode in the belly of a B17 or crouched in a muddy hole?

Our kitchen door on 17th Avenue Parkway looked out upon a long, narrow second-story porch just above the kitchen doorway. The chatter of English sparrows was a continuous music which emanated from this narrow porch. I decided to trap some of these intriguing birds as pets.

A long string led over the slightly raised window to my bed. I jerked the string and ran quickly to the porch to observe the results. Three sparrows were fluttering around, beating against the chicken wire of a cage about two feet long by a foot high.

I had decided that if I were to write a report on birds for school I should have a closer look at a wild bird. I opened the hinged front of the cage and a bird suddenly flew past my reaching hands. The front of the cage had been supported by a stick, and a path of cracked corn trailed from the edge of the porch to the cage.

This trap design resembled the standard bird bander's trap as described in an old 1928 article on bird banding found in the *National Geographic* magazine (2). The design had one shortcoming, however, in that there was no way to reach in and grasp the birds without opening the front of the trap. Later, I discovered I should have some sort of sleeve leading into the trap. A cage sleeve is a tubular piece of cloth tacked around a five-inch hole, attached into the back of the cage. It is kept closed with a rubber band. To retrieve a trapped bird one simply reaches the arm through the sleeve. My knowledge of the art of cage design was very limited. However, when I later became interested in insects I discovered that entomologists, who are the experts on cage design, invented the sleeve cage.

Perhaps because of the ability insects have for escaping from practically any confinement, ingenious entomologists have devised a whole series of cage devices. It was this ingenuity and down-to-earth character of the professional entomologist that led me along the path to become one myself.

At this time, however, I was more concerned with retrieving my two trapped birds. I grasped the second one in my left hand and headed for the basement where I had a six-foot-high aviary, complete with perches, built into a small storage room. I released the birds into the large cage, but contrary to my expectations they did not fly to the perches. Instead they began beating themselves violently against the screen wire. I kept the cage supplied with bread and corn, but despite great quantities of food, they refused to eat and one was dead the next morning. It was then that I learned that wild creatures taken abruptly from their natural environment are not easily calmed. I decided to release the other bird which appeared quite lively but was still of no mind to feed.

However, in order to have subject matter for my essay, I resolved to conduct an experiment so that my trapping project would not be a complete failure.

I had read in the *National Geographic* magazine article on bird banding that a captured bird can be hypnotized into not flying away by merely grasping it gently around the body and opening the hand slowly with the bird lying on its back across

Maggie, my pet, was taken from a nest along Sand Creek outside Denver, Colorado. Here Maggie sits outside my bedroom window. Every day I opened the window so she could come inside and sleep on a buffalo skull I had hanging on my wall. Neither buffalo skulls nor live pets in the house ever bothered my gentle and loving mother.

the open palm. The bird was supposed to lie quietly in this position for several minutes, eventually rousing itself to fly away.

The article was correct. The sparrow lay peacefully on its back, dormant in my palm for several minutes, with its eyes wide open appearing dazed or drugged. Suddenly, it rolled slightly to one side and jumped into the air. It flew around the basement, beating against the windows until I retrieved it and went to the yard to repeat the experiment. This time it remained even longer on its back, but after several minutes launched itself to freedom.

Years later a jackdaw fell down a chimney into the fireplace of a country inn where I was billeted in Ireland. I told some Irish friends of the strange type of bird behavior and they were somewhat skeptical. I took the jackdaw outside and demonstrated bird hypnosis for them. To this day, I do not know any good explanation for the peculiar response of a bird in such a position.

I completed my essay on wild birds by writing a short history of the English sparrow in America and ended it with my successful experiment. As I recall, the teacher was much impressed and my next two English assignments were on racing pigeons and training falcons. Both subjects were chosen by me.

Very early in my ornithological career I became much impressed by photographs of birds taken by Allen Cruickshank of the Audubon Society. I decided on bird photography as my next project, but before I was initiated into the difficulties of wildlife photography, I had an experience that changed my thinking concerning wild creatures.

East of Denver lay a broad expanse of flat, open prairie. This land, which has now gone the way of much such unspoiled country, later became the Lowry Air Force Base bombing range. It was at that time, however, the open haunt of the prairie falcon and the dainty little black and white lark bunting.

Often when I rode my bike the ten or fifteen miles into that inviting stretch of prairie, I would sight the graceful rough-legged or red-tailed hawk soaring on the early morning air currents. I owned a fixed-focus Jiffy Kodak which collapsed with a bellows. I soon discovered that no matter how close these soaring hawks looked in the view finder, when I developed my pictures nothing appeared but an unrecognizable speck. This is a common mistake of most neophyte photographers. If a photograph is taken too far away from an object that appears large to the eye, such as a distant building or mountain, the developed film will usually show little but the surrounding countryside or the foreground.

I was at this time the proud possessor of a BB gun. This is a gun about which to this day I have mixed emotions. With it my father taught me how to shoot and how to handle firearms safely, but the temptation to take pot shots at song birds was almost overwhelming.

Certainly evolution has ordained that man has within him an inherent instinct to hunt (3). Children from the Achuara

Western Meadowlark. The meadowlark is not a lark. In fact, it belongs in the blackbird family of birds also called a "meadow-blackbird." In spring it leaves the cover of the prairie grass, where it exists on seeds and insects, and flies to a telephone wire or fence post to sing. It has without a doubt one of the most beautiful bird melodies. It was just such a bird as this I shot. The meadowlark is distinguished by its bright yellow breast and black "V." The western subspecies sings a much more beautiful song than its eastern cousin.

village of the Amazon to the backyards of New York stalk the unwary feathered prey. The Achuara often, of necessity, stalk jungle birds because they are a part of their diet, but suburban children stalk because there is within them a subconscious instinctive calling.

At that time, however, for me a bird in the hand, especially one I could photograph close up, was better than a flock in the field. My first unfortunate victim was a beautiful yellow-breasted bird that I first observed out in my favorite prairie country. One was perched on a fence post, singing lustily, when I pointed the gun and pulled the trigger. The bird fell to the ground and fluttered away into the tall grass. I knew I had wounded it and ran excitedly toward the spot where I saw it disappear. I searched for ten minutes before I found my frightened victim almost fifty feet from the spot I had marked when it fell. As I reached down to pick up the bird, its tail feathers and wings spread loosely and its eyes opened and shut with a whitish flickering movement. I learned later that this was due to the nictitating membrane which acts as a protective sun shield over bird eyes. The membrane was flicking across the glassy eyes, the mouth was agape, and a trickle of blood ran down the white chin feather staining its bright yellow breast. I suddenly felt sick to my stomach, the same feeling I often experienced in our Model A when we made too many turns on the steep curves of a mountain road. Any idea of taking a picture with my Jiffy Kodak left my mind for what good was a photograph of a ruffled-up lump of bloody feathers? I began to hate guns with a passion and gave up the BB gun.

I found a picture of my victim in my little blue book of birds. The black "V" on the bright yellow breast identified it as the western meadowlark. I decided to take the body home and attempt to paint a water color picture of a meadowlark.

Perhaps, with the brightly colored feathers at hand, I could color a good likeness.

I had been experimenting with drawing and watercolors and had become disenchanted with the pictures of birds by Audubon. They always seemed to be stilted. I later found that this was considered to be true by many ornithologists. They attributed it to the fact that Audubon always drew from dead birds. The remarkable thing is that his pictures and observations were as accurate as they could be when one considers that in the early ninetenth century he had no field glasses to bring his subjects into close view.

In 1936 there appeared on the market the book that was to become my favorite of all the published popular bird literature. This was *Birds of America*, a large volume edited by Gilbert Pearson and illustrated with marvelously accurate watercolor plates by Louis Agassiz Fuertes. I was particularly impressed by his paintings of birds of prey in the second part of this book and spent long winter evenings attempting to draw and paint copies. I also obtained a volume entitled *The Hawks of North America*, by John Bichard May, from the Audubon Society, but considered the hawks in the plates by Allan Brooks too fat and puffed-up looking.

I was quite excited when, in a second-hand book store on Pearl Street, I found an old December 1920 issue of the *National Geographic* magazine with an article by Louis Agassiz Fuertes on falconry (4). I read the article and bound it together with my bird banding article in a folder. I was intrigued by the idea of getting a wild hawk to train myself. It was the first glimmering of a passion that was to continue unabated over the years.

Some of the earliest falconers have mentioned that a love for falconry is passed along from our ancestors and is not obtained by exposure to the sport from others. They say cer-

My friend Jon Harris finds a magpie nest in the Black Forest of Colorado. The nest is like a wooden fortress. The roof is thatched of heavy sticks. During the nesting season the tail of the mother bird can usually be seen sticking out of the entrance hole.

tain people inherit a love and a way with these intriguing birds. If so, one of my ancient Irish or Spanish forbearers might have served as chief or assistant falconer to the court of a Gaelic king or Spanish monarch. Perhaps he flew his charges at rooks or herons along the winding bank of the Erne, over the rolling moorlands of Donegal, or hawked grouse along the foothills of the Pyrenees near the castle of the Ainsas.

Ainsa is a village in Argon in northern Spain. My mother is an Ainsa, descendent of a family that came in royal Spanish galleons to California by way of the Philippines, then migrated to El Paso, Texas. She has told me of two brothers that each received a ship from their noble family. One sailed to the Philippines and the other to South America to seek their for-

My first drawing (watercolor) of a bird of prey. The rough-legged hawk appears on the snow-covered prairie of eastern Colorado between October and March. It migrates from the summer breeding grounds in Canada at such heights that it is seldom seen until it suddenly arrives over our prairies. It is often seen perching, as in my painting, on a tree stub or fence post. It hunts low with claws down and head "hanging" as it searches for field mice It is 100% a rodent eater and the farmer's best friend. Despite that fact, in my boyhood, I saw as many hanging from fence posts as in the air hunting — hopefully times have changed.

tunes. Perhaps the one that came to America, after being attacked by pirates and shipwrecked in the Philippines, had with him a brace of falcons. At least I would like to think that he once hunted in the foothills of Aragon, flying his falcons against the backdrop of the snowy Pyrenees. At any rate, there seemed to lurk within me a deep unreasoning desire to learn all I could of this sport of kings, as Fuertes called it in his article.

I somehow reasoned that hawks and falcons ate birds as naturally as we ate cows and chickens. God willed it. If eating birds were natural, I equated shooting them for fun with original sin — it was one thing to raise birds for food, quite another to kill for fun.

I spent my early teen years searching for hawk nests along Sand Creek east of Denver. I never found one, but I did find dozens of huge stick magpie nests. They were roofed over with heavy branches. I climbed to many for sparrow hawks, now called kestrels, were supposed to nest in deserted ones. I was delighted as the beautiful blue and white mother magpie always sailed off, resembling a floating feathered cross.

I still remember the meadow lark that died with a red "sacred heart" on the breast, and the sparrows that died of fright and starvation. I had learned about death and dying at a very young age.

CHAPTER II
A Hawk for the Bush

*I do invite you tomorrow morning to my house
to breakfast; After, we'll a-birding together.
I have a fine hawk for the bush*

Merry Wives of Windsor, *Act III, scene iii, line 243*
William Shakespeare

My search for hawk nests along Sand Creek near Denver proved fruitless. There were plenty of nests in the tall cottonwood trees along the creek, but they were magpie nests.

When I learned my family was moving from Denver to Detroit, I quickly climbed to one of the huge, roofed nests and obtained two scraggly looking bobtailed birds for pets (1). Later in Detroit, these birds escaped and made the *Detroit News* front page:

Hungry Magpie Decamps While Its Pal Grieves

Amateur ornithologists in the vicinity of the Detroit Golf Club are concerned about the disappearance of a magpie which left its sorrowing companion to face the winter in solitude.

Corporation Counsel John P. O'Hara reported the mysterious disappearance of the bird and the singular behavior of his companion Friday.

About two months ago, O'Hara recalled, his son John, Jr. first saw the two birds, distinguished by long tails and black-and-white plumage, disporting in the O'Hara preserves at the rear of 17580 Fairway Drive.

O'Hara's law partner, Frank C. Cook, who lives at 17390 Fairway, reported that a few weeks ago, while shaving, he heard a tapping on the window. He saw on the sill one of the magpies, apparently hungry.

Cook hurried to the kitchen and emerged in the yard with food. Before he could set the dish on the ground, the magpie alighted on his shoulder, he said. The bird was tame as a chained macaw and almost as hungry, he reported. The other magpie also enjoyed the feast.

On Tuesday one of the scolding magpies was missing and the other, apparently saddened, prepared for the winter by burying part of his food in the yard, marking the spot with a leaf which he pressed over the cache and pierced with his bill, to make it stay in place.

O'Hara thinks that perhaps somebody trapped the other bird for a pet.

O'Hara was correct. Maggie and Jiggs were my noisy long-tailed pets. I let them fly free in our backyard but they strayed further and further away.

I went to the lawyers yard and collected Maggie. I never saw Jiggs again and assumed that he drifted away into the local golf course woods. Maggie was a wonderful pet and, throughout the year we lived in Detroit, slept every night on the horns of a buffalo head given to me by the Denver Museum of Natural History.

The author at age 15 with an eyas (young) kestrel. The kestrel is actually the smallest member of the falcon family. It was, in my boyhood, called a "sparrow hawk." It lives in farm country and hunts the crops and grass for mice and grasshoppers — a farmer's good friend. It is one of the few birds that can hover in place and in ancient Egypt was the sign of Horus the falcon sungod — levitation!

My father soon informed us we were moving again. He had been transferred to Menands, New York, near Albany.

Our new house sat at the edge of the beautiful Sage estate belonging to the railroad tycoons of the Eastern establishment. We had left Detroit with my Denver magpie and also with a baby Cooper's hawk, called in falconry terms an *eyas*. A Cooper's hawk is a short-winged accipiter hawk which hunts in deep woods. I had taken the little ball of down from a nest in a tall hardwood near the edge of Detroit.

As summer approached, I was about to attempt my first hunt with Caesar. As is the case with most beginning falconers, I was in dread of losing my bird. I could see him flying off over the forest never to return. I said a few silent prayers so as not to suffer the fate of an empty-fisted falconer.

The road through the Sage estate led along the edge of the high fence, turned by the old barn, and followed the margin of a large open field. The field lay on the edge of the rolling hills that form the steep drop-off into the Hudson Valley. From the top of a hill, where the field surmounted the Hudson River Valley, I could see as far as Troy in the north, and south to the wooded farmland across the river. In early morning, the haze rose from the river and mixed with the smoke from the factories along the river banks. I would start out early, carrying Caeser on my fist, skirting the edges of the field, and looking for feeding English sparrows to hunt. By nine o'clock, the sun had burned the haze from the river. The far away whistle of the New York Central train directed my gaze to the silver streak of tracks that wound along the east bank of the river. Through binoculars it looked like a toy electric train as it puffed along towards Troy.

When I first started hunting along the wooded edge of the field I would begin very early, for this is the feeding time, when birds come out in numbers. It is the best time for hunting and bird watching as the calls of the feeding birds can be heard coming from the fields and woods. Another reason for my early morning walks, however, was fear that the owners of the estate would chase me from their property.

One morning, leaving the open field and following the road into the woods, I met a lady and man on horseback. They stopped me and the lady asked what kind of bird I had.

"A hawk for the bush, ma'am," I replied.

"Hawk for the bush" was Shakespeare's description for the short-winged English sparrow hawk in *The Merry Wives of*

Caesar, my first hunting bird. It is believed falconry began over 4,000 years ago in China. Caesar was not a falcon, but rather a short-winged accipiter or wood hawk. Falcons, like the peregrine falcon, hunt in the open. Accipiters, "short wings," hunt in the forests. Thus Caesar was ideal for hunting the woods and fields of Menands, New York. I obtained this bird as an eyas male from a nest in a woodlot at the edge of Detroit. The leather straps are called jesses.

Windsor. At that time we were covering Shakespeare in third year literature. I had gone through several of his plays looking for falconry jargon.

"Hawk for the bush? What on earth is that?"

"I am a falconer," I replied proudly, "and I train birds of prey to hunt."

"What are you hunting here?" she asked. "Not my pheasants, I hope." At that time the Sage's were releasing pheasants on their property, as I well knew because I had put many of these beautiful gold- and rust-colored birds in the field.

"No ma'am," I replied emphatically. "Caeser could not take a bird as large as a pheasant, and besides, I would not hunt someone else's pheasants. Caeser is good at catching English sparrows and they eat the grain from your pheasants' pens," I added hopefully.

They questioned me more about falconry and rode on without a word about my hunting Caeser on their property.

About two months later, I lost Caeser and despaired of ever seeing him again. I had flown him at a sparrow near the bridge across the creek that flowed through the estate, but the sparrow escaped into some blackberry bushes. Caeser put up into some tall pines in the woods and wandered off. I had miscalculated his keenness (2) to hunt. In about a week the Sage's caretaker came to our house with Caeser stuffed in a gunny sack.

"He chased a sparrow into our garage," he said, "and we knew from the straps on his legs it was your bird." I thanked the caretaker profusely and happily returned Caeser, none the worse for wear, to his bow perch.

Today as I write this, I am thankful that I grew up in the '30s and '40s when adults were less suspicious of the young, and also far less likely to chase them off their land. I feel deeply for the young today. Simple things such as love of God and love of nature are not often instilled. Most schools today teach not love of nature, but love of control and management of nature. We try to improve on God's work by computer models of what nature is thought to be. Many assume that God is a myth of Christians and the Bible a mere history of Judaism.

While living in Denver I was in and out of the Denver Museum two or three time a week. Children of today could not afford that educational privilege. Today the entrance fee is $3.00. The museum was a path to nature for those closed in by brick and asphalt. I think one of the most descriptive phrases ever coined for our non-designed cities is asphalt jungle.

It is wise, before flying a hawk at quarry, to offer her a bath. Hawks love to bathe and preen themselves, and are very particular with regard to their personal hygiene. On a hot day, after an unsuccessful flight, a bird that has not had a chance to bathe might wander off in search of water or a stream for a bath. My failure to furnish Caeser a bath might have been why I lost him the first time.

One day I was placing his two-inch-deep bath pan in front of the bow perch when a flash of wings attracted my attention. A little male sharp-shinned hawk shot out of the backwoods in hot pursuit of a robin. The robin twisted and turned, but the little hawk followed every dodge and overtook the circling robin on the open lawn beside our house. A bird of prey that has just killed will seldom start plucking and eating immediately, but will hunch over the dead prey for a few moments, as if guarding a long lost treasure. At the kill, the wings are half-spread over the quarry and the back feathers are ruffled out with the tail partially spread sticking out behind. One claw is usually closed like a vice around the victim's head, and the other dug into the back. After a short wait, the hawk will bend over and start plucking the prey, pulling out feathers in gobs and shaking the beak from side to side to rid it of the sticking

Diana, my first hunting peregrine falcon. I took her from Haystack Mountain, Vermont, the summer of 1946. I hunted with her through September, when I released her in order to sail for Japan as a civilian radio-range technician. Here she has brought down a pigeon and is plucking her prey. The eastern peregrine is now nearly extinct thanks to the scourge of mankind: insecticides, like DDT. Peregrine falcons are now on the protected species list, and only a master falconer can own one. Attempts are being made to reintroduce the Canadian subspecies in the eastern United States.

down and coverlet feathers. Once in a while, the crouched hawk will lift its head to look around and scan the surrounding terrain for its mortal enemy, man. At such times, the eyes will glare in defiance from under the deep brows which are a distinctive characteristic of birds of prey.

The sharp-shinned hawk suddenly caught sight of me and quickly flew off from its prey. A wild hawk will seldom leave the prey for long; it will invariably watch from a distance and return as soon as the coast is clear. This habit can be used to trap wild hawks which have been observed on the kill. The falconer chases the bird off and surrounds the kill with small upright stems or some of the flexible feathers from the prey. These are stuck in the ground, point first, with the flexible end pointed up and a noose is put around the circle of feathers, being held about three inches above ground level by the feathers. The falconer then runs this long cord to a place of concealment about twenty yards away. When the hawk returns to the kill, a quick pull on the noose will slip it up around the hawk's legs which are holding the prey.

I decided to try to trap the wild sharpie in this manner and ran the long string to the garage window. The hawk returned, but I was too excited and pulled the noose tight prematurely. It closed around the dead robin instead of the hawk's feet and he flew away like a bullet across the road and into the cemetery. I reset the noose and waited for two hours, but he never returned.

Since it was June and he was a mature male, I knew that his nest must be somewhere in the surrounding woods. I searched the large estate to no avail, and on the next weekend decided to try a large, wooded area across the road from the estate which was known locally as Witches' Woods.

Witches' Woods was a large tract of hardwood and mixed conifers broken only by a string of steel power-line towers that bisected it. At one corner was a U-shaped lake called Little's Lake used as a swimming hole by the local children.

In the winter, when the trees were leafless, I would hike through the snow-covered woods spotting each tree that contained a stick nest and marking the location on a geological survey contour map. The woods were a place of solitude in winter, and only the crack of ice-burdened trees and the chick-a-dee-dee of the little black and white eastern chickadee would break the early morning silence on those grey winter days. Sometimes, if I were out late enough in the evening, the wolf-

wolf of the great horned owl would float through the woods as the sun went down. The dry, cold of the winter air, the grey skies, and the chickadees and nuthatches moving about on the leafless tree limbs imparted to the winter woodlands a sort of melancholy but appealing bleakness.

In spring, the warblers passed through on their migration, and I got my first glimpse of the gaudy little redstart searching the tree tops for newly emerged caterpillar and spider egg sacs. Early spring was the bright time of year, and the leaves of oaks and birches were a light delicate shade of green that furbished the whole forest canopy. The early morning sun shining on the dappled leaves and the painted redstart flashing his red-edged tail and coverlets in and out of the concealing green foliage furnished the visual backdrop for the many bird songs that filled the morning air.

During the spring, I made the rounds and visited all the nests I had plotted with such care during the winter with no success. One Saturday while walking back down a ravine through which ran the small creek that drained Little's Lake, I passed a thicket of hemlock trees. Suddenly, an excited cluck-cluck-cluck came from above. I looked and saw a little sharpie sitting on a limb, pumping his tail up and down, and making excited clucks toward me. I found some whitewash on the lower limbs of one the hemlocks and, by moving around from side to side with my field glasses, could barely make out a small stick nest thirty feet up in the air in the crotch of the middle tree of the grove. It was so well concealed that I had missed it in my earlier winter searches. The sharpie nest is somewhat easier to find that the Cooper's hawk nest because the little hawk is extremely noisy during the time the young are in the nest and almost always gives itself away by its loud clucking and flitting about in the nearby trees.

I returned the next day with my climbing irons and Jiffy Kodak loaded with film. I wanted to get some pictures of the young in the nest. The first limbs of the tree were quite low, and the Kodak folded up fairly flat in my pocket, so I was able to reach the nest with little difficulty. There were four downy eyasses in the "cotton" stage that preceeds the pinfeathers that blossom out later. They were still in the eyas-like position of sitting back on their haunches, and they backed to the edge of the nest and cheeped defiantly at me. The nest was quite loosely woven around the edge, and three of them backed away until I thought they would tumble through the gaps in the small sticks. One small male remained crouched in the center, and no amount of persuasion could induce him to join his brothers and sisters at the edge of the nest.

Eyas sharp-shinned hawks in their spruce tree nest 40 feet above the forest floor. This was the nest I photographed with my first Jiffy Kodak camera. It was necessary, with such fixed focus cameras, to lean far out from the tree to get three of the eyasses in focus. Note the one in the foreground is blurred.

The Kodak had a narrow depth of focus, and, as I was hugging the tree trunk, I could not get back far enough to get all the little hawks in focus. For my Kodak to focus, I had to back off at least five feet, but there was nowhere to go. I finally solved the problem by tying a rope around my waist and around the tree trunk and leaning back as far as possible. I was still too close and had to settle for pictures of the three at the edge of the nest. I clicked off the entire roll, ignoring the eyas in the center of the nest. I was so engrossed in my picture taking that I did not notice the mother bird flying silently from tree to tree and getting closer and closer to the nest. Finally, with a loud clack-clack, she swooped down from a limb above and darted past me like a flash. I could understand why this hawk has been nicknamed the little blue darter. She swung around and flashed by again, this time closer, and I could feel the backwash from her wings brush my cheek (3). Having made her displeasure clear, she flew up to her perch and scolded me even more vociferously. Her reddish orange breast, slate blue back, and fiery red eyes seemed to be symbols of her defiance and courage, and I felt quite ashamed for upsetting her domestic tranquility. Had I not happened by she would, no doubt, be sitting contentedly with one leg pulled up under her feathers, waiting for the cool of the late afternoon to hunt, for hawks seldom fly in the heat of the day.

I climbed down and took some pictures of the grove of hemlocks to illustrate a typical nesting area of the sharp-shinned hawk. I still have that black and white photo of nesting sharp-shinned hawks on my wall.

My whole boyhood was full of love and happiness because I was blessed with parents who understood the needs and wants of children. Though my father was a military man, he fully approved of my love of nature. He was an agnostic, however he kept me pointed toward a love of God and nature. My brother Eugene, my sister Ann, and I were educated in Catholic schools at considerable expense and hardship to him.

I was, at that time, one of approximately thirty practicing falconers in the entire United States. In 1941 I helped found the American Falconer's Association. I had become an authority on birds of prey. It was a paradox of my life that I, who detested guns and killing, became a practitioner of a sport dedicated to killing birds.

I soon learned that a modern falconer takes very few prey. The famous ornithologist, Arthur A. Allen, in *The Book of Bird Life*, points out that quarry that fall to hawks and falcons are usually sick or old. Birds of prey are God's way of keeping nature fit.

A falconer cannot train or manage a falcon or hawk; he can only work with the behavior and skills that God instilled in the bird. The falconer learns about the physiology and behavior of his hunting companion in order to mesh his desire for "hawk watching" with the desire of the bird to feed, preen, perch, or climb high into the sky. The hunting falcon controls the falconer, not vice versa. The competent falconer knows that. Pseudo-ecologists who criticize the sport do not, and, even worse, many never get to know God through nature.

My love of hawks taught me as much about God as it did about nature. I did not realize it at the time, but it also helped me to survive war and terrorism. Hitler and Divine Providence were to make of me a radioman — a deadly occupation in time of war.

CHAPTER III
Radioman

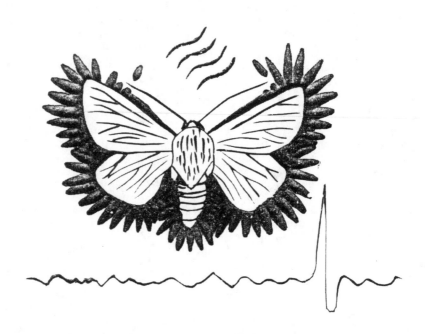

Much tension here this Sabbath, Schuschnigg had a secret meeting with Hitler at Berchtesgaden, but we don't know what happened.

Berlin Diary, 1934-1941
Vienna, Feb. 13, 1938
William L. Shirer

The coffee hut was near the operation office on the flight line. The early March day was bright, and we could watch as various planes landed and rolled up on the taxi strip. I liked the C47's best. They were the military version of the old commercial DC3 and were the real workhorses of the Air Corps troop carrier command. They were large enough for heavy hauls but small enough to be flying airplanes. Unlike the giants and the later jets, they could glide on the wind. One felt that they were metal birds, and that the pilot was flying and controlling their every motion. They had a roar to their engines that I loved to hear. When the ignition was hit, they would cough and sputter a couple of times before starting with a resonate vibrating thunder that filled the cold crisp morning air. Even from miles away I could distinguish a C47 warming up for a flight.

When they wheeled around, little eddies of dust kicked up from the taxi strip near their tails. Because the tail rested on the ground, the props washed the runway close to the plane. Puffs of smoke from the exhaust and dust from the runway seemed to be part of a living, vibrating thing about to leave the earth. The more modern planes, with their tails off the ground and their powerful props or jets, merely blast a path far back down the runway, too far away to be part and parcel of the plane's total character. I say character because the C47 always seemed alive to me. I wanted badly to ride in one. I was in the Army Air Corps, but had never been off the ground (1).

Instead of flying, I was spending my last months of training at a low-frequency radio range school at Chanute Field, Illinois. Chanute Field was a well known Air Force training center. It was my last electronic radio school in 1944, and will always be a magic place in my psyche. Once in a while, in almost every life I believe, there comes what I call a flash of happiness — a fleeting moment that must be what heaven is like. It is so powerful that in that instant one knows the supreme joy of God. No evil can exist. I have had two such flashes. The first occurred sitting at that coffee shop on an Air Corps taxi strip watching those graceful olive colored C47's taxi up. A strange place for a feeling that must mimic the beatific vision on a lower scale (2).

After finishing radio range school, I went to Godman Field at Fort Knox, Kentucky. Godman was a transfer point and replacement depot for Army Airways Communication System (AACS) personnel. There I helped to wire-up equipment in the control tower, but was soon on my way to Baer Field at Fort Wayne, Indiana. I spent the rest of April at Baer Field at a transmitter site. The transmitters were remoted from the control tower at the edge of the runway, and were set up in a cornfield about five miles from the runway. Each shift, I would report to the line, pick up a weapon carrier to drive out, and relieve the maintenance man on duty at the site. Someone had to be on duty 24-hours a day, so we rotated the night shift.

Baer Field was a Troop Carrier Command assembly point where hundreds of the olive drab C47's landed and departed for overseas bases. Their departure crews, wearing brown leather jackets, flight caps, .45 pistols, and jungle knives on their belts, were the envy of those remaining behind. Most were taking their planes to England in preparation for the great invasion of Normandy. They did not have the range to fly directly, so faced a long and hazardous flight southward across the jungles of South America to Natal, Brazil. From there they flew across the Atlantic, landing on Ascension Island for refueling, then on to North Africa and northwards to Italy or England. They followed low-frequency radio beam stations like the ones I had been trained to maintain.

On a three-day pass I decided to go to Terre Haute, Indiana to visit my aunt one weekend. Terre Haute was where my father grew up, and I wanted to see this southwestern Indiana town.

I took the train to Indianapolis. While I was in the station changing trains, I heard a New York Central train announced for New York City by way of Buffalo and Albany. I knew I had never been in the Indianapolis railroad station before, but I suddenly had that strange sensation that comes, one time or another, to almost everybody. I was overcome with the enveloping feeling that at some previous time in my past I had been in this very spot, and that what was happening had happened to me in the past. It is the feeling that gives some credence to the Buddhist belief in reincarnation. It is an odd sensation called *déjà vu*. The feeling is strong and exhilarting, and can sweep over one in the most unlikely places and times. As I pondered the feeling and listened to the train announcements for Albany, I suddenly changed my mind about Terre Haute and bought a ticket for Albany, New York, where my mother and sister were living. Not a smart thing to do as there were MP's on the train and my pass was for 50 miles and three days, not for 500 miles. With help from above I outwitted the MPs.

Perhaps my father had passed through that station many times before me. I have often wondered if genes, which can transmit physical characteristics from one human to another, might also be able to transmit certain pieces or bits of mental information, perhaps by exact duplication of logic or memory circuits in the brain from one generation to another. It does not seem entirely unreasonable that at least a portion of a child's brain might exactly duplicate that of a parent and in the process carry bits of stored information across from parent to child. We know that on the lower level of insects that instinct — *knowledge* might be a better term — for certain behavioral patterns are transmitted from generation to generation.

This photograph of Belleek, Ireland was taken on July 17, 1944, fair day.
On the 17th of each month, the County Fermanagh farmers would drive their
cattle, horses and sheep to town and bargain in the main street then celebrate, of
course, in one of the four Belleek Pubs.

Certain butterflies, such as the red admiral butterfly of
Europe, migrate over great distances from North Africa to
England in the spring, where they lay eggs and die. The next
couple of generations remain throughout the summer in
England, changing their stages from egg to caterpillar to
cocoon to adult. Finally, a late summer generation takes off
and returns to the same spot in North Africa from which its
forefathers, two generations before, had departed. Surely this
is the inheritance of information, for the butterflies have gone
through several generations existence as plant-feeding cater-
pillars before the final generation of butterflies leaves on the
long flight southward. How does this last generation remem-

ber the direction home to Africa? Perhaps if we could answer the mystery of how this stored complex of navigational information is passed on from generation to generation, we would be able to better understand some of the puzzling aspects of our own behavior.

In April my orders came to proceed to McClellan Field near Sacramento, California. McClellan Field was the port of embarkation for the Pacific Theater, as was Fort Dix in New Jersey for the European Theater of Operation. At McClellan I boarded my first C47 for a hitch-hiking ride to Reno, for a fun weekend.

I had hardly turned in my parachute when I was called to headquarters, given shipping orders out of New York harbor, and transportation orders for a troop train eastward. My shipping orders read "cold, wet and windy." I was very close to cursing God. If there were such a thing as Divine Providence, as is believed by most Christians, how could God conspire to send me, a bird lover, to the Arctic where the only birds were Arctic terns and snowy owls.

I was certain I was headed for the far north because I knew the Army Airways had a string of weather and radio beacon stations that stretched from Great Falls, Montana across the Artic through Greenland and Iceland to Scotland (3). I landed at Liverpool after a week-long trip aboard the huge oceanliner *New Amsterdam*. I ended up at a replacement depot at Stoke-on-Trent in the midlands of England.

A week later I was in the far west of Ireland at a radio station with the call letters of WXVP. Its secret name was Belleek Radio Range, and it had become a key navigational aid for American aircraft making landfall over western Ireland. It was also utilized by the antisubmarine flying boats of the RAF Coastal Command. It was the primary beam station for the Battle of the North Atlantic.

Of RAF Coastal Command, Winston Churchill said, regarding the U-Boat menace:

> At the same time, however, we gave orders to the RAF Coastal Command to dominate the outlets from the Mersey and Clyde and around northern Ireland. Nothing must be spared from this task. It had supreme priority. The bombing of Germany took second place. All suitable machines, pilots, and material must be concentrated upon our counter-offensive, by fighters against the enemy bombers, and surface craft assisted by bombers against the U-boats in these narrow vital waters.

For two years I was the only radio technician keeping the station on the air twenty-four hours a day

On a warm day in July, as I sat in the sun by the door of the radio station, my attention was held by a specimen of a beautiful red admiral butterfly as it danced across the green turf and landed unerringly on the yellow blossoms of a solitary plant. Overhead a giant RAF Sunderland flying boat banked gently over the station, and, with silver wings flashing in the sunlight, headed straight down the river for Lough Erne ten miles to the east. Soon the crew would be sipping tea in the mess. Perhaps I would run into some of them in an Enniskillen pub that evening. As I watched the butterfly and listened to the drone of the Sunderland fading to the east, I was struck by the homing ability of both the man-made machine and the butterfly. Besides wings, I thought, they have in common something called antennae. It is hard to find out exactly when the term antennae was first applied to the thread-like appendages of insects. I believe they were named for the radio antennas and not the other way around. They had originally been labeled feelers. It may have been their resemblance to the wire Marconi was stringing about on Salisbury Plain that prompted some early entomologist to label the insect feelers antennae. The derivation of the word antenna is Latin. It comes from the medieval Latin term *antennae*, meaning sail yard. Marconi's experimental antenna farm must have resembled a sail yard,

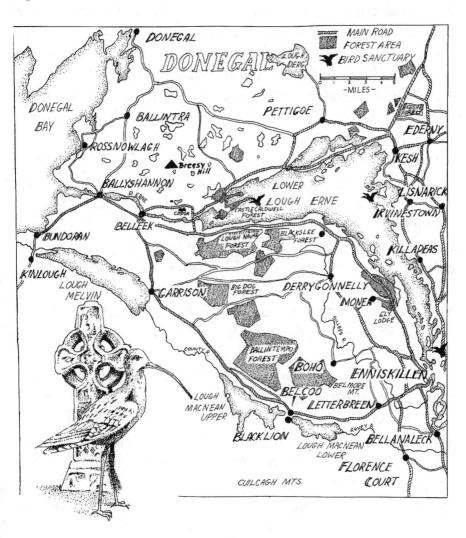

Map of the Irish countryside around Belleek. Belleek Radio Range was in the bend of the road by the castle just east of Belleek. Lough Derg is the large lake just at the top of the map. Breesy hill was my favorite granite mountain. I often climbed to its summit to think, and for a little peace and quiet. The Catalina and Sunderland flying boats landed on Lough Erne near Irvinestown.

with wire strung in all directions. The radio range station in Ireland certainly resembled a sail yard with long loops of wire crossing each other.

The RAF Sunderland submarine patrol depended on the range station, and the flying fortress arriving from the States picked up the beam several hundred miles out at sea and followed it to Prestwick, Scotland. A breakdown of this low-frequency radio station might spell disaster for the Air Force crew. Over the ocean on a dark and stormy night, it was the difference between safe landing and being lost at sea. Just as unerringly as the aircraft located my station, the small red admiral butterfly had homed in on the lone yellow flower. True, the butterfly probably saw the yellow flower and headed straight for it, but seeing it is after all electromagnetic communication. Yellow is just as much a frequency as is 300 kilocycles, the frequency of the Air Force radio range station. The difference, of course, is that the wavelength of yellow is only 0.57 microns long (a micron is 1/1000 of a millimeter), whereas the 300 kilocycle wave is about 3,000 feet long. Quite a difference in wavelengths, and between the two lie 35 to 40 octaves of the electromagnetic spectrum. Despite the fact that the butterfly probably located the flower by sight, what about the antennae? Of what use are they in locating host plants and other insects? More especially, what about night-flying insects such as moths? Do they find their host plants and mates by visible radiation? Had my red admiral butterfly used his antennae, to identify the plant by some electromagnetic radiation generated by the plant? My interest has always been birds, but as I speculated I added insects to my list of subjects to be studied when the war was ended and I returned to college.

The night shift at the station began at 7:00 p.m. This is long before the sun sets in such northern latitudes, Belleek being 54 degrees 34 minutes north, putting it close to

Repairing insulators on the Belleek radio antenna. From 80 feet up, a good view is obtained of the Irish countryside. The border between north and south Ireland runs down the center of the field just in front of the Irish cottages. Below is the fuel shed and our jeep. My companions, both radio operators, stand below.

Newfoundland latitudes on our continent. In early summer it is usual to see sky light as late as 11:30 p.m. Often in the late spring and summer I would hear a peculiar sound filling the evening air over the station. I searched the sky for the source of this sound as it was so regular that I soon came to associate this faint drumming of the late evening sky with spring in Ireland. I was certain it was a bird, but had not the remotest idea as to its identity. Like the wind through the beeches and the looming bulk of the castle, it too had a certain haunting connotation. When I inquired from old Mr. Gormley as to the source of the drum-like whispering noise, he informed me that it was a heather bleater.

It was weeks later in Londonderry that I finally located a book on British and Irish birds. During the war such books were out of print and difficult to obtain.

From the book I learned that the heather bleater is the local Irish name for the common snipe; the snipe that closely resembles our Wilson's snipe. I had never heard this sound from the American snipe, but later learned that it is produced during mating season. During its evening flights from the surrounding marshes and boglands, the snipe climb high into the air and fall in steep, oblique dives. During its display flight the snipe produces the almost bleating "huhuhu" by the vibrations of its widely spread outer tail feathers.

If from books I learned about nature, then from Ireland and the Irish on the border I learned about why fear of famine, and political murder are easily overcome by faith and prayer.

My life in western Ireland was much more primitive than life in the United States. We lived well on cabbage, tea, meat, eggs, and bread, but could obtain none of the foods in wartime Ireland that we were used to in the states. There were no plumbing facilities, and to keep warm we had to constantly attend our barracks fire. One might say our standard of living was low, yet by my own estimate it was the ultimate paradise that I had settled in. I was close to the land and the people that worked the land. Surrounding me were miles and miles of wild moorland, mountains, bogs, and isolated loughs nestled like sparkling diamonds in the purple mantle of heather, bog myrtle, and antler moss. The curlew and red grouse inhabited bogs that stretched for miles and miles above the cliffs that bordered the shore of Lough Erne. It was possible to hike all day and not meet a single person or see a house. At evening, returning home, the ever present drumming of the heather bleater above would remind me that the hills of Ireland had become my home.

God certainly knew my wants when he changed my orders from the Pacific to Ireland. Later thoughts of my "madness" at God for sending me eastward were humbling, for in Ireland I was as close to God's paradise as anyone alive can ever be.

CHAPTER IV
On The Border

Many of the Cistercian houses of English foundation were violently anti-Irish and many forbade the reception of any Irish as monks. The Irish complained to Pope John XXII in 1318 that the Cistercian monks of Granard (Abbeylara) and of Inch declared it no sin to kill an Irishman and would even celebrate mass after doing so.

Lough Derg, Legendary Pilgrimage
John B. Cunningham

Cleary's Hotel is located at the end of the wide main street of Belleek (1). The main street approaching from the north appears to dead-end at a large, imposing cream-colored building with several wings and steep sloping gables. This is not Cleary's Hotel, but rather their competitor: Elliot's Hotel. Cleary's is on the east side at the end of the street where the road takes a sharp turn around the corner and passes on towards the pottery before turning right again and crossing the ancient stone bridge that, in those days, humped across the swift flowing River Erne. The bridge was exceedingly narrow and impractical as its sides were constructed with high stone balustrades. There was room for only one car at a time to pass. As with things impractical, the bridge was exceedingly charming and contributed greatly to the scenic beauty of this exquisite town. Alas, as with most things both charming and impractical, it was also later destroyed and replaced by a concrete monstrosity. At the time, however, one could speculate as to its ancient origin, for the stone balustrades along its side were constructed such that there were three triangular niches off each edge. This type of construction is found in only the most ancient of bridges, and the side niches served the pedestrian as safety step-asides during the inevitable emergency, when the helpless foot traveler was caught in front of the galloping horses of the stage coach or local militia.

The card advertising Cleary's Hotel stated that it was both tourist and commercial and was "most central for fishing, shooting, and visiting all the local places of interest." It further stated, "visitors who come once will call again and recommend it to their friends." With this statement I was inclined to agree, if not for the comfort of the inn, which varies with the coldness of the day, then most certainly for the gentle and kind people who owned and managed the establishment. If one were to list all the virtues that a traveler or visitor to a strange land might wish its inhabitants to possess, then certainly leading any such list would be the virtue of kindness.

The stranger deprived of kind and hospitable treatment by unthinking locals soon becomes both suspicious and cynical. The Irish, renowned both for their hospitality and ability to converse on most any subject, produce very few cynics among their visitors. Because of the harshness of the Irish rural life one might expect harsh treatment, but the opposite is the usual in Ireland. The Irish are often moody, gay at one moment, melancholy at another, but those moods are softened with a lively humor and love for their fellow man. If love is the real basis of Christianity, then Ireland is surely one of the most Christian countries.

The Cleary's, being no exception to the traditional Irish character, were more than patient with the eight Yanks who invaded their small hotel. The family group consisted of Desmond Cleary, the proprietor; Mary, his wife; and his partially handicapped sister Amanda. Their three-year-old son, Jimmy followed the Yanks around, forever turning over their cups of tea, or otherwise acting exactly as a three-year old is expected to behave. Another member of the family was Bridget. Although to all outward appearances a maid, Bridget had spent her entire adult life with the Cleary's and was, to be more precise, a member of the family. Jimmy was the "apple of her eye," consequently, he could do no wrong.

Bridget represented the last of a disappearing type of European woman for whom there is no comparable replacement in our modern world. She was faithful, hard-working, and born to the land as if her body had been moulded and cut from the rocky hillsides. In truth, her apparel, often smeared and dubbed with the black soot from the turf fire, or her brogans, covered with manure and bits of grass from the pasture where she tended the cows, attested to her closeness with the land. During the late summer haying season she could rake, stack, and thatch the ricks of hay to the shame of any man. Some of my friends thought her dirty, but bred of the city they mistook the warpaint of man's eternal agricultural battle for uncleanliness. In fact, there are two types of dirt: dirt of the soil, without which man cannot survive, and dirt of character, in which the selfish and hard of heart wallow. Bridget was, in fact, not unwholesome, but saintly in her unselfish devotion to others. Because she was simple of heart and spoke with the ancient brogue of the Donegal hill country, some also considered her somewhat less than intelligent. Again, nothing could

Typical thatched roof cottage — McGee farm. Each room has an open fireplace. Turf (peat) fires heat the house in winter. The limestone walls and thick thatch keep the home warm in winter and cool in summer. This is one of the most energy efficient houses ever invented by man. The kitchen-dining area is in the middle with bedrooms on either side. The McGee home is larger than most Irish farmhouses, and 13 children were raised here — all healthy.

have been further from he truth. Bridget knew the techniques of her hostelry and agricultural trades, and seldom wasted time on the senseless or unnecessary.

We ate on the second floor of the hotel at a huge oaken table, in a room that served as both a sitting room and dining room for the establishment. Against the outer wall, between two windows overlooking the bridge and river, was the fireplace. The chairs with their backs to the turf fire were, by any measure, an ideal spot. The cold chill of an Irish winter can only be overcome by toasting one's backside at the turf fire. In the early days at the turn of the century and prior to the war, Cleary's was filled with Scottish or English fishermen on their fortnightly holiday. The River Erne was renowned for both its trout and salmon fishing. During the war, however, times became hard and only a few commercial travelers would stop at the hotel. Invariably, at dinner time they sought to seat themselves by the fire, and just as invariably, Bridget would shuffle through the door with tea and intervene to reserve the favored chairs for the Yanks.

"Shure oi'll be after seating ye in this place, shure oi've fergot entoirely to tell ye, this one's Mr. O'Callaghan's place at ta toime."

The big event on fair day in Belleek was the dance in Johnny McCabe's hall that started promptly at nine p.m. It usually featured a local ceili band consisting of a set of drums and three fiddlers. The ceili dances are the traditional dances of Ireland and resemble in many respects our square dances without the calling. Square dancing is in fact derived from the Gaelic ceili dances. Some of the dances are quite involved and go by such picturesque names as the Siege of Troy, the Walls of Venice, and the Walls of Limerick. They represent in dance and music Ireland's old and continuous battle of independence from England. Interwoven with the ceili dances were such physically exerting ones as the Scottish Highland Fling and the slower modern foxtrots of the late 1940s. The fiddlers were good and considerable energy could be expended during a few dances. Since the hall was small and none too ventilated, bod-ies were somewhat closely packed and the haze from cigarette smoke rather dense.

The system for meeting and selecting a dancing partner or for flirting with previous or newly won favorites was simple yet sophisticated beyond any modern folkways of matchmaking. Since the hall was small, its walls could be furnished with only a certain arrangement of benches. After each dance, and before calling another, these benches were taken up mainly by the men, thus leaving little space for the remaining girls attending the dance. The arrangement might seem very ungentlemanly to the stranger, but was not intended to be so, for it left the girls a considerable variety of laps to sit on. Since a lap is obviously much softer than a hard wooden bench, the solicitude for the ladies at the dance was evident. The system had several further built in advantages as a social custom. First, since all the girls were sitting on laps, no one girl could be considered foreward and, secondly, it is extremely difficult not to strike up a conversation with a lady sitting on your lap. It was extremely easy to find out exactly who was who about the countryside for the Irish are not well acquainted with inhibitions that make for non-conversation. There was one last advantage to the "system" as I call it. Since the benches were hard and extremely narrow one was in continuous danger of sliding off, and this eliminated any danger of excessive courting behavior among the precariously perched couples.

There was, however, one disadvantage to the Irish system of matchmaking, and this was that it discriminated against the newcomer, especially a newcomer from across the sea and in Yankee uniform. The Irish country people, in spite of their

The author across the border in civilian clothes. Ireland was not neutral during the War; I crossed the north/south border regularly. I could have been interned. Some trips were for pleasure, *e.g.* my future wife and I near Sligo town on a picnic. Some were unofficial business, things like assisting the search for flying boats that crashed in southern Ireland. Pilots were always returned to their squadrons across the border in North Ireland. Germans were interned.

great love of America and Americans, were no different than people of any other country with respect to the soldier. A soldier is, after all, a soldier, and well understood to be less inhibited than the average citizens who are not subjected to the unknown and fearful that are part of the soldier's lot. Parents the world over simply do not want their daughters associating with strange men in uniform. If one of our Yanks should occupy a bench, it would take a considerable amount of courage for an Irish girl to perch herself on his lap. No one really likes to be different, and this would certainly give her a reputation of being forward, for no one can deny that a foreign uniform is different. The consequence of this was that we Yanks were most often seen leaning against a wall of the hall not wishing to appear ungentlemanly (by our own standards), and not entering into the merriment at all.

It was several months before I worked out a system that enabled me to join the Irish "system." This consisted of buying tickets from the lovely girls who peddled them around the benches. By never missing a dance (I could trade my night shift to Wee Rocky who was married), I soon got in enough words to become acquainted with a few of the girls. From then on they lost their aversion to the Yank lap, and things progressed normally. The dancing was fun, the music haunting, and that the system worked well is attested to by the fact that the Irish girl who most often sat on my lap was named Winnie. She became my bride a few years later in New York.

I became acquainted with a young Irish man, tall, gaunt-looking and of my own age, named Marty Keegan. We soon became very close friends. His plans were to join the seminary and eventually become a priest. Because he was plagued with asthma he had not been able to pass the rigorous physical requirements for life in the seminary. He was the son of a schoolmaster at a local school. We would often bicycle with his father to the school, and then continue on to the rocky coast road. Marty had friends at Kildoney Point, and these men battled the winds along this rugged coast, setting their nets from small boats for the green, speckled herrings. The fish were then peddled at stands in the surrounding Donegal towns on fair days. Sitting on the rocks after a day at sea, we would plan our future after the war. Across Donegal Bay the rugged peak of Slieve League rose in the distance. St. Columbkille must have missed this rugged mountain land when he left for the great monastery of Iona in Scotland. The Irish coast was too beautiful to leave without sorrow. We often spoke of St. Columbkille, and how he was responsible for the spreading of Christianity across Scotland and England from Iona, the great center of religion in Western Europe.

Marty hoped that the days spent rambling over this wild and restless land, combined with exposure to the sea breezes, would help his asthma (2). I went on as many bicycle trips as possible with Marty, and immersed myself in photographing the intricate rock structure of the Donegal Coast. It is the rocks that contribute so much to the scenic charm of Donegal. The cottages are of rock, the ditches are also rock, and thrusting up from between the green and brown fields or hanging suspended on the edge of sea-sprayed cliffs, are rocks, rocks, rocks. There are all varieties of rocks from the common limestone, from which farmers get lime for white washing their cottage walls, to complex mixtures of igneous rocks thrown into long folds and ridges stretching in waves across the land.

The fall weather soon became rainy and cold. The sun seemed to drop from the skies faster each day as winter approached. Although early in the war, there were four MP guards and three radio range operators at Belleek Radio Range (besides myself the only technician). We were ill-equipped to defend ourselves from a submarine landing party, or the very small group of fanatic IRA trained by the Germans. The latter entered Ireland by submarine and parachute (3).

The fact that we were attached to the RAF Coastal Command Base at Castle Archdale on Lough Erne did not endear us to a few local IRA types. Concern about attacks were relayed to us by phone and were well documented on paper at RAF headquarters in England (4). By December, 1945, the MP's had left, and most of the interned IRA had been released.

I was the lone radioman left at the station. It became a time of mental disquietude.

The Cleary's often invited me to stay with them overnight so I wouldn't have to spend the stormy nights out on the haunted grounds of Magheramena Castle. The old parish priest died in the castle and willed his telescope to me. The grounds were considered doubly spooky now. Besides the ghosts, there were the RAF warnings. I kept my service .45 handy, as the wind whistling around the barracks at night created a setting right out of *Wuthering Heights*. When one is alone, whispering branches, pelting rain, and shadows cast by a fire from a small stove can produce an abundance of frightening apprehension.

My bunk was on the south side of the barracks beneath a set of elongated French windows that opened inward. One night I began dreaming of the ghost of Magheramena Castle. The dream soon resolved itself into the ghost of Magheramena barracks as I became aware of a resonate thump-thump-thump.

Colors began to flash through my dream. I could see the green lady of Magheramena pounding on the shutters of an old, broken-down cottage. Suddenly, the cottage blew up in a terrific explosion, and I was being set upon from all sides by sinister-looking men in caps and mud-caked Wellington boots. They began firing, and the thump-thump of the shutters changed to the rat-a-tat of a machine gun. I grew hotter and hotter until I suddenly began to suffocate. Something was trying to drown me, to force my face down into the warm mud of a turf cut. I threw off the stifling covers and rolled out of bed onto the floor, half awake and half asleep. I had suddenly became aware that someone, or something, actually was trying to choke me. I realized with a terrifying shock that this was no nightmare, but the real thing. The two submachine guns assigned to the station were locked in my foot locker. Maybe my feelings about the Irish were all wrong. Maybe the IRA really were after the weapons, and this was their chance with only one person on duty. I did not take too much stock in ghosts, so it had to be the IRA. As these thoughts flashed through my mind, I was suddenly wide awake. I rolled across the floor to a chair where my .45 hung in its holster. As I drew it out and slammed back the breech to jam a cartridge home, I noticed something white coming through the French window above my bunk. The window was wide open, and the rain and wind were blowing in, throwing the window back and forth against the wall. I raised the .45 because nobody was going to get those machine guns without a fight. As I took aim, my assailant suddenly snorted. I looked closer and suddenly sat back down in my chair with a tremendous feeling of relief. I was trembling, but started laughing because through the window protruded the damp head of a black and white cow. The wet nose and hot breath was directed down above my pillow. Somehow the cows had broken the strands of wire that fenced the barracks, and the whole herd had gathered around the barracks.

One cow had pushed my slightly ajar window further open, and was sheltering her head from the storm. I drove the herd out, sat down, and made myself a pot of coffee. I have never before or since thought myself so close to death, nor asked with such fervor the protection of my guardian angel.

CHAPTER V
Some Unsolved Mysteries

In this tradition (Irish), there is a trust in the objects of sensory perception, which are seen as signposts from God. But there is also a sensuous reveling in the splendors of the created world, which would have made Roman Christians exceedingly uncomfortable.

How the Irish Saved Civilization
Thomas Cahill

Life at Magheramena was becoming lonely, especially during the long winter evenings. I spent more and more time at Cleary's Hotel, sometimes talking far into the night. If it was too late, I would stay at the hotel, and sleep in the back room that overlooked the bridge and the River Erne. The bed was big and comfortable, and the rushing sound of the water from the river gave the room a special quality of peacefulness. Sleep came easily as it enfolded one with a kind of tranquility. This seemed to be a part of the paradox of the whole Irish countryside. A nostalgic, melancholy, beautifully tender, yet colorful land whose very characteristics in many ways appeared to contradict the violence and discord that for centuries kept the country in turmoil. A revolutionary violence that was still to be felt ran deep beneath the surface and was only glimpsed in the bitterness of some of her people toward the English.

Sometimes, under pressure of keeping the complex radio range transmitters on the air twenty-four hours a day under somewhat primitive conditions, I wished for the brains and common sense of Dorothy and the novel character of the Scarecrow in the book by Frank L. Baum, *The Wizard of Oz*. I considered that tale equal to any of the marvelous Irish fairy stories I heard visiting around the countryside (1). It is the great example of a realistic and natural women's liberation written long before those words appeared.

For two years I had watched as transports and bombers flying in from the coast of Ireland had picked up the west leg of our Belleek radio range station. Winging their way up the Erne valley north of the fog-shrouded Leitrim mountains, they headed for England and battle. Some of these planes and crews perished in flames over Germany, and those who did survive had long since passed westward on their way home. A few transports and RAF patrol planes still used the station, but it was only a matter of time before orders would arrive to close it down

After VE day I was assigned as NCO in charge of the station. Within a few months I commanded only myself. The station operated on a three-day a week schedule, so I planned a trip to Dublin while I still had the opportunity. Jim Shute, an RUC Special Forces Officer, and Joe Duffy, both of whom were friends, accompanied me.

From Eden Quay we caught a bus and crossed the Royal Canal and the Tolka River skirting the Irish sea to the picturesque town of Howth. As we crossed the Royal Canal I wondered how far it went and if it was still in use. It is shown on most maps of Ireland and connects with the Grand Canal that crosses Ireland to the Shannon (2).

At Howth, a sleepy seaside town of steep streets, we dallied for about an hour over a cup of tea at a quaint little tea house overlooking the sea. I had heard from an Irish ornithologist that there were good bird cliffs on Ireland's Eye island. I swam across the one-mile distance while Jim and Joe rowed a boat across. The sun was bright, the water warm, and in no time we were pulling the wooden dingy ashore. Ireland's Eye got its name from the fact that it sits like an eye in the bend made by the peninsula of Howth and the mainland. When I visited twenty years later it was swarming with tourists and bathers, but just after the war, we had the entire island to ourselves.

Still standing on the island are the walls of an old chapel with a leper window. The chapel was presumably built in the 7th century by the Sons of St. Nessan, an order of monks. Tradition has it that lepers coming to the chapel were given food, or observed the mass through these so-called squint windows which were built to give the worshipers a better view of the altar.

The word leprosy is derived from the Greek word *lepra* (*lepros*) meaning scaly. The order of moths and butterflies are called *Lepidoptera* as they are covered with scales. There is now considerable evidence that the so-called leper houses, found throughout medieval Europe, were nothing more than food shelters for the sick and poor.

Above the rock cliffs along the edge of the island, a group of black-winged birds were adding sound effects to the usual seabird orchestrations. Nature's music seemed to have been especially composed for this eventide on a seaside cliff. Several of the birds hung suspended in the air, at times almost immobile except for the heads which turned from side to side, until like giant fluttering leaves they settled with repeated strident cries of kyow-kyow-kyow to the rocks. These were the lesser black-backed gulls. They had probably nested along the cliff tops earlier in the season.

I turned my glasses to view the leper church far below. Today the bacillus of leprosy is almost as much an unknown as it was centuries ago. Unfortunately, such a fear and fog of superstition and myth have grown up around the word leprosy that even in our modern day world an unbiased and rational approach is almost impossible. It is one disease where public thinking is far behind medical knowledge. The fable that it is highly contagious lingers on probably due to biblical descriptions of leprosy in the Old Testament. To this day we know nothing about how it is transmitted, and still do not have a cure. It can only be arrested.

The heather on the island was alive with many species of butterflies. My collection of Irish butterflies was getting quite sizable, but was rather ragged since I had no net and caught many of them by hand. Over the years I have mentally thanked my younger sister Ann for turning my mind to entomology. Years before, when she needed a school science project, she asked for my help. Together we decided on a butterfly collection. Often I would capture a good specimen by sneaking up and throwing my cap over the insect. In a secondhand bookstore in Belfast I found my first good, beautifully illustrated insect book, *Butterflies and Moths of the Countryside*, written and illustrated by F. Edward Hulme in 1903. Not only were his paintings of butterflies and moths masterpieces of art; his text was informative and readable.

Science, especially nature writing, seems to have reached a peak of insensibility and dullness today. The paralytic and numbed prose of enumerated facts flow from the pages of journals, both scientific and amateur, like sand from a dump truck. The poor reader is barraged with such dry, unfeeling sentences and tedious tables of statistics that he soon loses his excitement for the life of the subject matter. Woe betide the scientist or graduate student who uses a feeling sentence or dares to speculate and theorize in his discussion at the end of a thesis. The fear of anthropomorphism or mention of God is so great today that descriptive words, or words with emotional connotations, are rejected.

One of the rarest butterflies of the British Isles is the Bath White. This beautiful mottled white and yellowish-green species is highly prized by collectors in the British Isles. It is extremely common on the continent and as far east as Japan. Where its English name, Bath White, came from is unknown since it is most often taken in southeastern England and not on the western side where Bath is located. Perhaps an early entomologist did capture one near Bath. Usually only one or two specimens are captured each year in England, but in 1872, 35 specimens were netted. In 1945, the second year I was in Ireland, 650 specimens were collected. The Bath White is easily captured since it is usually seen flying slowly and close to the ground. It settles to the ground often between short flights.

How is it that an insect weighing less than a gram can leave its home on the continent and beat its way across the English Channel and St. George's Channel to arrive safely on the coast of England or Ireland? Better yet, why do insects migrate, and why are certain years more favorable to these long-distance flights, while at other times few, if any, are collected? What was there about 1945 that caused over three times as many Bath White specimens to be collected in England and Ireland during that one year as had been collected for all the years from 1850 to 1955 — over a century of collecting? Had the great war on the continent somehow or other affected the continental population and set off the great migration?

I was slowly being drawn to a study of insects in somewhat the same manner that I was drawn to birds. The interrelationships of nature were becoming synthesized in my mind. I was developing from my reading an understanding of the relationship existing between the flora and fauna of the countryside, and the physical forces that governed their existence. Ecology, the study of the relationship of living things to their total environment, was a fast-growing branch of biology. I had already decided that when I returned to college I would become an ecologist, but I still thought my main interest lay in the study of bird life.

I knew about the effects of weather on life, and I began reading in other fields. In 1945, Ellsworth Huntington published his *Mainsprings of Civilization*, a penetrating analysis of how climate, diet, geography, and heredity controls the character of an entire nation and helps to shape its history. His chapter on cycles and rhythms was fascinating, and later, as I traveled around the world, I observed with startling regularity the truisms of many of his deductions about the development of human civilizations. I never ceased to wonder, however, at

The large Basilica of St. Patrick on the Island of Lough Derg. Pilgrims in the foreground rest while while in the background barefoot pilgrims cross the small stream on the island. They are saying the rosary as they walk the "stations." Stations are the round rock foundations of the Monks' ancient "beehive" huts or living quarters.

the almost perverted evasion of any mention of God. The mindset of modern materialistic science is that something comes from nothing.

Not long after returning from Ireland's Eye, Marty Keegan and I were sitting around the turf fire in Cleary's Hotel discussing the the famous Irish pilgrimage to Lough Derg.

"Shure," Desmond Cleary said. "Yourself and Marty should go on the pilgrimage to Lough Derg now that you can cross the border in uniform."

The pilgrimage to Lough Derg was called by the Irish "St. Patrick's Purgatory," and I had heard about it from many people around the countryside. On August 6, the great war ended, and an American bomber flying over Hiroshima in far away Japan had bequeathed to mankind a disquieting future. I thought it might be a good time for a few prayers, and, besides, it was certain to be a new religious experience for me. The pilgrimage to Station Island in Lough Derg is perhaps the most rigorous in our modern world. Legend was that St. Patrick spent time there in prayer. The name of the lough is derived from the Gaelic Dearg or Red Lake. Since the early days of Irish Christianity, it has been not only the most rigorous, but in all probability the most popular of Christian pilgrimages. It ranks with Lourdes in France as place of devotion for Catholics, but it is not as well known except to the Irish. Few Catholic Americans have ever heard of Lough Derg, yet most are well acquainted with Lourdes in France (3).

Early one warm August morning, Marty and I were on our bicycles, peddling to the train station in Ballyshannon. From there we caught a train to the little border village of Pettigo situated four miles from Lough Derg. The border between Northern Ireland and the Free State runs down the main street of the village, and it is the crossing point for pilgrims. At Pettigo travelers from Dublin and most of Southern Ireland converge to catch the bus to Lough Derg. In olden days the pilgrims, many very old, walked barefoot over the rugged hills of Donegal to the Lough.

As our bus topped the last hill beyond the little crossroad hamlet of Ballymacavany and dropped steeply through the mountains towards the Lough, I became increasingly awed by the melancholy beauty of the surroundings in this desolate stretch of moorland. All around us the sides of the heather-covered hills were bathed in a translucent haze, and the top of each stone shone saffron yellow against rain-swept darkened clouds. Ahead, in the grey haze of light, lay a dark body of water dotted with rocky islands enveloped by a misty shoreline. To the east I could see beautiful Kinnogoe Peak, which faces across the rock-lined lough towards Croagh Breac, its rocky neighbor to the west. In the distance, the great stone basilica appeared through the morning mist. Nestled in the wild surroundings as naturally as the little water grebes that swam about the surface of the lough, the basilica rose from the waters as if it were placed there with loving care by the hands of the Almighty. I was suddenly aware of the enveloping quietude and tranquility that must have attracted the great Irish Saint to this solitary lake island fifteen centuries before. If the great apostle of Ireland should descend to the rock-strewn sides of Croagh Breac to wander the shores of the silent lough today, he would find no encroachment of modern civilization to alienate his meditative spirit.

Tradition has it that St. Davlog founded a religious house on another island. He started the pilgrimages to Station Island where some of his sedentary monks lived in Celtic "beehive" stone huts. This type of hut was typical of the earlier period of Celtic Ireland. The remains of these cells are still on the island and today are called "beds."

We descended from the bus at the edge of the lake and stood in groups. Soon, a large, wooden boat propelled by two long, bulky oars approached. The pilgrims piled into the boat until approximately 150 were packed in tightly. Little room was left for the rugged-looking countrymen who pulled the oars. Although there was a steady breeze across the choppy lake, the oarsman made good progress against the whitecaps. Soon the details of the basilica came into view. The huge bulk of the Hiberno-Romanesque basilica sits atop a craggy knoll at the edge of the island, like a mesa rising from the shimmering lake of a desert mirage.

On landing, the pilgrims are obliged to remove their shoes and stockings and spend the next three days walking barefoot while making what are known as the stations.

The first night on the island is spent in an all-night vigil in the basilica, chanting prayer after prayer. At first, the continuous sound of Aves and Creeds is monotonous, but it soon becomes hypnotic in effect. Eventually one becomes hauntingly aware of a certain close communion to the spiritual and to God. Chants and repetitious prayers are a method of communion used throughout all ages. Whether in Catholic monastery, Buddhist temple, or at a Baptist revival, the effect is always one of the fusion of the mass consciousness into an almost unified state of exhaltation. The whole mind eventually seems to focus on the spiritual, and the monotony of the words decreases with time. Monks chanting the Litany of the church in the solitude of a resonate chapel, and in the still of the night, represent the pinnacle of this type of communion. At first, one becomes sleepy to the degree that it seems utterly impossible to remain awake, but as the prayers stretch into the night they are broken occasionally by intervals of relaxation outside the basilica. Breathing in the cool air that blows across the island from the surrounding hills kept the eyelids open when the weariness had gone beyond endurance.

The three days spent on the island passed quickly. On the last night we were given a bunk in one of the station hospices. The hospices are starkly plain, whitewashed buildings provided with numerous basins for washing the dirt from one's bare feet. Our sleep was the sleep of the just, as nothing could equal the delicious feeling of a mattress after the long burden of fatigue from days and nights of prayer and fasting. The one meal per day could be taken at any time, but since it consisted only of black bread and sweetened tea we usually postponed it until the end of the day. By then it took on all the attributes of

Misty photograph of the huge oar-powered boat coming back from Lough Derg Island. Legend has it that St. Patrick did penance on this island or the smaller island close to it. The beautiful basilica can be seen across Lough Derg in the distance. Lough Derg means "red lake," and it is also known among the Irish as St. Patrick's Purgatory because of the hardships of his three-day pilgrimage. Today, modern technology has taken over, and the boat is now motor powered. Thus the wonderful silence of these wild moorlands has been desecrated. Apparently the modern Irish are too frail to pull oars. For an excellent book on the subject read *In the Absence of the Sacred,* by Jerry Mander.

a banquet feast. In spite of the cold wind blowing across the island, the fatigue, and the bare feet, no one has ever been known to leave the island with a cold. Although no cures are claimed for Station Island, as at Lourdes, this of itself would seem to be some form of miracle. Even Marty's asthma took a turn for the better. On the island there was a prevailing silence, as no speaking was allowed. It lured one into meditation in almost the opposite manner as that of chants in the basilica at night. It is this sort of communion with God and Nature that is most amenable to my own nature. Although I was surrounded by crowds, because of the silence, present life seemed unreal and thus all the more spiritual. It is an overpowering experience to be a part of a mass of humanity and yet have perfect solitude. It is this paradox of crowded solitude that contributes so much to the spiritual environment of a place like Lough Derg or Lourdes and other such holy places. Modern civilization, with its noisy crowds, rebels against such an environment and is the poorer for it. The closest one can approach such inspiring solitude in our American cities, with others present, is in the reading room of the library. Perhaps that is why I enjoy them so much. In later years, when I was cut off from the fields and woods in New York City, the reading room of the library became my favorite city place for meditation.

On departure day, after the final station, we gathered again at the little landing and were sent on our way refreshed with tea and hymns of the remaining pilgrims. The boat pulled slowly away from the dock, the heavy oars dipping softly in the water.

For the first time, I began to understand the simple faith of these Irish Catholics and to wonder at the strange, mysterious hold that such holy places have on the human psyche. The biggest mystery of all, of course, is Jesus Christ who lived 2,000 years ago near the shores of Lake Galilee.

CHAPTER VI
Leper's Rock

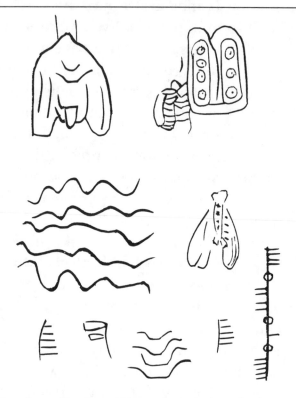

People who suffer from Hansen's disease suffer both bodily and emotional hurt, but of the two the blow to the spirit is more traumatic, or the more shocking to mental life. There is the shock of knowing that one is afflicted by what is perhaps the most chronic of all diseases, from which recovery, even at its quickest, can be hoped for only after months, more probably years, of treatment. Besides, they have heard of all the horrible deformities that attend this disease under its traditional name "leprosy": the Biblical cry "unclean, unclean," rings in their ears.

N. Carl Elder, Resident Protestant Chaplin
PHS Hospital, Carville, Louisiana

The sun beat down with scorching light. It warmed the back of my neck like the embers from cow dung fires that warmed the mothers cooking breakfast along the road. My friend Irwin Pless and I had skirted the edge of New Delhi and were hiking beyond the tall sandstone Red Tower, the Quib Minar. We had passed by the elegant tower, and decided to visit later in the day.

As we walked in the early morning sun, a beautiful black and chestnut colored hoopoo, the magic bird of India, flew up from a weed field. It was a vision of soft orange-brown against the yellow and blue flowers of the colorful field.

I wondered why some plants are dammed and called weeds when in actual fact they are flowers. In fact, I later learned that weeds are a friend to the farmer, not his enemy. They send their roots deep into the soil, and drag the trace elements and minerals needed for healthy growth to the topsoil surface.

In my opinion, weeds were not accursed any more than were the poor and often hungry Indian villagers. Neither should the poor be considered outcasts, or weeds, by the richer, more blessed humanity of the world. It seems that although Christ time and again revealed His love of the poor and sick, the well-to-do despised the poor then as now. Ask any politician.

As we left the Quib Minar behind, I viewed in the distance across the brown grassy plain, a rocky hill fortress and deserted mosque. It rode the sweeping waves of brown desert grass like a huge sailing ship above the horizon. It was on that hike to the deserted fort that I once again questioned my plans to study birds upon my return to college. Birds were my great love, but I asked myself, "Would not the study of agriculture be more helpful to a starving world?" My mind was haunted by sights of wretched, starving, bodies laying along the sidewalks of Calcutta.

Irwin and I had left Japan where we both worked as electronic technicians for the Air Corps, and were traveling the world with backpacks. We were the first of what would later be called wandering "hippies," or so we would have been labeled in the early '60s.

We had escaped from Communist overrun China with the Flying Tigers. We lived with the elephants and mahouts of Northern Siam (as it was then called), and hiked the hills of what was later known as the Golden Triangle of drug lore. In Siam we visited the leper colony on the Island of the White Elephant. It was situated on an island in the river Ping near Chiang Mai. The emperor had once kept his sacred white elephant there. By 1948 it had been turned into Siam's leper colony. It was there that I first learned the sociology of that disease — and the horrors (1).

The sociology was contained in one word — banishment. If it could not be cured, ignore it and banish the victims from all contact with humanity. It was, and still is in fact, an immune factor disease with the same plot of ignorance and fear as present day AIDS — a later disease I was to become very familiar with. It is also a disease with far more victims today than ever existed in the time of Christ.

The New Testament is filled with stories about Christ's affection for lepers. They are my favorite stories, especially the one where ten were sent to the High Priest for a cure approval and only one returns with a "thanks."

The New Jerusalem Bible calls leprosy a "skin disease." It is an attempt to relieve the mental anguish of the sickness. It is not a skin disease, it effects all parts of the body, and would be better called an immune system disease for the single reason that 80% of the population is immune to the attack of the bacillus. Thousands of years after the gentle Christ walked the earth we still do not know why some people are not immune.

In *Matthew 8:2-4* and *Mark 1:40-44*, Christ cures a leper, and then cautions the blessed man not to tell anyone — an impossible request, as Christ well knew, for an ecstatic patient. What joy in Christ that cured man felt. He babbled it all over the countryside assuring that the God-Man Christ would be kept busy. Luke's story about the ten cured and one returned (*Luke 17:11-19*) points out the second greatest sin of mankind's ingratitude. The first, or so it seems to me despite all the dwelling on "sins of the flesh," is hypocrisy.

How many people, I wonder, ever thank our trash collectors — we would be buried in refuge but for them. The postal service is usually badmouthed, as are farmers. What if they all, in justice, decided to quit? That would be a national disaster on a par with total war.

It is the administrators, stockbrokers and generals who are usually thanked. Some deserve it and some do not. Wars are fought by privates, sergeants, and lieutenants around mistakes made by most (not all) generals. Christ loved farmers, prostitutes, laborers and centurions (lieutenants) — not bankers and generals. Maybe that should tell people who profess to be Christians something. The lepers of Leper Rock certainly told me a lot about such things.

As Irwin and I approached the ancient deserted rock, we could see huge black pondercherry vultures perched in rows along the ridges of the curved dome of the structure. They resemble living versions of the gargoyles found on western cathedrals with one difference, they were the garbage disposal system of Leper's Rock and also undertakers — nature's way.

Irwin and I understood from Indian friends that hundreds of such deserted village forts dotted the dry semiarid plains of northern India. They had been deserted since the sixth and seventh centuries when Mogul warriors from eastern Asia rode out of the rising sun and overran India. If city Indians thought

Deserted mosque way out in the desert north of Delhi, India. Black ponderscherry vultures and lepers were the only inhabitants of these sad deserted villages. Bottom: Round fortress tower and rocky outcrop of this ancient fortress village. These fortified villages were overrun by the Moguls in the 5th to 8th centuries. The black ponderscherry is the most common vulture in India.

such places, built among desolate rock outcroppings, were deserted they were badly mistaken. Most were non-government sponsored leper colonies.

The village was a series of steplike terraces of red sandstone rock outcropping. It resembled the red sandstone of the Qutb Minar. The angular fractures of the red rock were connected by man-made stone walls which ended at a round tower resembling in many ways the monk's round towers of Ireland's monasteries. The huge domed mosque rose high above the walls and tower-like structure.

As we drew closer it was almost impossible to tell the people sitting listlessly among the rocks from the huge black vultures. On the side from which we approached was a large, flat, table-like area of rock. Two Indian women in dirty saris flailed stalks of millet lying in piles between them. Their heads were covered with cotton mantles so their ears were not visible. I could see that one lacked a nose. Leprosy attacks the cold body parts first, fingers, ears, nose, etc. We had obviously stumbled on a village of outcast lepers. It was a scene right out of the movie *Ben Hur*. Times never change.

We climbed up the sandstone cliffs to a point above the stone wall and round tower. As I climbed I could feel surges of energy fill my body. Later that day, climbing the steps of the 234-foot-high Qutb Minar, I seemed to absorb the same sort of energy. It was a feeling I almost always attained climbing the steep sandstone or granite cliffs where falcons have their eyries. Despite a long day hiking, I returned to Delhi as if I had just risen from a good night's rest — I had experienced the magic of stone.

I was not thinking of the Virgin Mary at Leper's Rock, but sometime during my world journey it slowly came to me that two elements of nature's character are almost always associated with the apparitions of Mary — rocks and birds. Rocky places are common — Kerrytown in Ireland, Lourdes, Fatima and Medjugorje in Yugoslavia. The image of Guadalupe was formed on a rocky hill to the songs of numerous birds.

I remember that on my long walk in the sun I visited many of Mary's special hills, and in tight spots said my share of "Hail Mary's." I am quite certain she often comes to my aid as surely she does for all who ask.

Sometimes our Catholic devotion to Mary is taken in the wrong light. One does not pray to Mary, or her icon, but rather recalls her closeness to her Son. We ask an intercession to Him for help, or give thanks for blessings rendered as in the case of one leper returning to thank Christ (2). It is a very simple concept no different than asking for a letter of recommendation from a friend's mother.

In fact, it is such a logical and pleasing way to pray that I was surprised when certain American bishops went out of their way to downplay Mary's roll in spiritual life: the arrogance of scholarship. May I ask why so many churches, including my own, have moved the Holy Family from either side of the altar cross, and at a time when the priests preach family life? Why, even in Ireland, the rosary is now seldom said by families in the home? When I returned last year to Belleek, Ireland, the church was being remodeled. Mary's statue was moved to new wing where she is hardly visible to the flock. One would need a guide to find her icon in a modern church. Change is often for the best, but it can just as often be a disaster. Burning flags develops from a lack of respect for the traditions of one's country; moving Mary out of sight is the same phenomenon, besides being anti-female.

It was while reading about the life of Father Damien, who was isolated with lepers at Molokai, that I first really learned the power of prayer through the rosary.

It is well known that the mass kit he loaded on his horse, for a rough mountain trip, held a few extra rosaries. As soon as he arrived he gathered the the unfortunate for benediction and rosary.

I have carried my rosary since childhood, and at least seven times I survived certain death because of my love of Mary and my belief in my guardian angel. Perhaps it is a childish belief for one classified as a scholar, nevertheless I hold it a truth beyond question — more so than any scientific theory in any book written by the greats of science.

Irwin and I spent several hours on the rocky knoll that protruded from the windswept Delhi plain. The inhabitants, most of whom seemed to have leprosy, were unusually happy for a people so afflicted. The two women flailing the millet seed smiled at us as we passed by.

We entered the great dark mosque. Inside it was cool and a place one could easily take a long nap had not the been floor littered with bat guano. A few lepers did doze inside its vaulted innards. Like the rocky hill, it seemed filled with a strange vitalizing energy.

I was to feel the same energy in many ancient structures as I traveled the world over the years.

I believe those people of Leper's Rock to be far more at peace with their lot than the fretting lepers of the Calcutta streets. They were, or so it seemed at the time, an almost normal functioning group.

Most certainly the rock was a "magic" fertile spot on the semi-arid plain. In places, trees grew out of the sandstone rock. The rock was surrounded by green millet fields almost as if, in the endless land, it sent energy, not only into the lepers, but also into the soil. At Leper's Rock I was beginning to have the glimmer of an understanding of the faces of God and nature in rocky places.

Usual to such rocky places where people gather, are pictographs, or rock writings. I searched the rocky walls and terraces but found none left by the centuries of leper inhabitants — their thoughts are not of posterity.

At Carnak in France, and at numerous Irish stone monuments, I have copied in my notebook pictographs of insect forms and waves of energy (see chapter heading block cut). On one rock at Carnak was carved an insect antenna.

Insects often sun themselves on rocky tors (See *Tuning in to Nature* by the author). Insects, like the *Leper bacillus*, have a waxy covering. I was soon to become as interested in the power in wax as I was in the power in stone. Why do waxy covered insects like to sit on the hot surface of energetic sun heated rocks? Plants are coated with a micrometer (1/1000 of a meter) thin layer of wax. What was the connection between plant wax coatings and the energy emitting "light" of the rock from which plants often sprouted? Why is the *Leper bacillus* coated with a protective layer of wax?

The disease is as enigmatic as it is baffling. The bacillus *Mycobacterium leprae* is almost indestructible. In later years I became interested in wax as an electronic substance called an electret. It became the main focus of my home experiments concerning the strange leper bacteria.

Dr. Philip Draper, a British researcher, has pointed out that the leprosy bacilli could not be grown and experimented with in the laboratory until some way to culture it under laboratory conditions existed.

Sometime in the 1970s, researchers, in particular a nun at the U.S. Public Health Hospital at Carville, Louisiana, began experimenting with, of all creatures, armadillos. They succeeded in infecting one animal with the bacilli in its foot pads. In a short time, they were able to culture millions of the bacilli from the fleshy ears of the armadillo. Dr. Draper is quoted as saying that the study of leprosy is like walking through a bog.

Today with special drugs leprosy can be controlled, but not cured. The bog is a little less dangerous, but as Irwin and

Two leper women on a flat rock flailing millet. Millet grows very well in the dry semidesert soil around such rock outcropings. The stone mesa acts as a paramagnetic antenna to collect the magnetic energy of the environment and retransmit it to the semidesert around the rocks. The mosque and round towers certainly amplify the energy making for better growing conditions surrounding the rocky fort.

I walked back across the the grassy plain toward the red tower, I resolved to find out exactly what the ancients knew about the energies of stone and the mystical properties of wax. Perhaps that night in New Delhi I would find a Catholic Church and light a wax candle in front of an icon of the Virgin Mary. A very pagan accomplishment the uninformed of our materialistic world would suspect.

My Search for Traces of God

PART II

God and Physics — Divine Providence

Christian mysticism is not the rather ludicrous mysticism so prevalent in our materialistic civilization, but rather a simple mysticism which recognizes that God created nature, and that He can manipulate it as He sees fit. In short, a miracle is not supernatural because it contradicts nature; instead it is supernatural because God wills it in order to further enlighten us, and to inspire a strong love for Him and creation.

The Shroud
Philip S. Callahan

CHAPTER VII
Form and Frequency

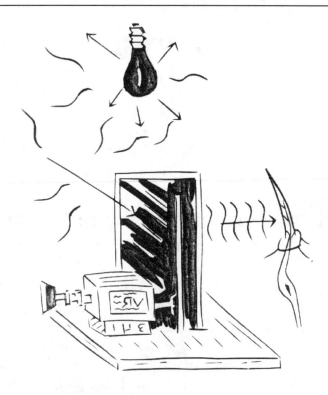

"*I suppose you are an entomologist?*"
"*Not quite so ambitious as that sir. I should like to put my eye on the individual entitled to that name. No man can be truly called an entomologist, sir; the subject is too vast for any single human intelligence.*"

The Poet at the Breakfast Table
Oliver Wendell Holmes

It was nighttime. I pulled the big box of wooden matches from out of the tin case. As I struck the match I wondered why there were so few books on the history of light? The oil lamp, and later the candle, changed civilization during ancient times, even up to the Roman Empire, as no other technological advance except the wheel. The American Indians, including my favorite Pueblo, had discovered neither.

Chico Canyon, the largest Pueblo of all, believed to exist between the 10th and 15th centuries, produced no oil lamp remains as do the ruins in the Middle East. Indian Kiva were lit by sunlight through open windows and camp fire.

Candles, or so it seems to me, are like lasers. Their sharp-edged flame against atmospheric space indicates weak resonance — like a radio in tune.

There is absolutely no way to drift into the meditative, love-state of God as easily as spending a few minutes before an image of God's mother Mary fronted by flickering votive candles. One can fall into the arms of Jesus through His mother and the magic of candlelight within seconds. It is even better than going to "grouchy" old priests in confessionals, although "grouchy" old priests are also a blessing.

Both votive candles, in front of icons of saints, and priests were God-inspired strokes of genius. I will always be thankful for them.

Strangely enough, during the early years after I returned from my wanderings around the world, the "beat generation" of poets and writers such as Allen Ginsberg, Jack Kerouac and William Burroughs (of the famed cash register family) understood candles and the confessional with one big difference; their inspiration was taken over by evil, and they vulgarized everything they touched by falling for the sickness of hedonism. They slept with every willing individual and confessed it to the world. The hippies followed suit, and in both cases it was drugs and liquor that scrambled what might have been saintly brains.

The evils of the two Ds — drugs and drinking — can never be underestimated. God has left us better ways to quell our fears, and they are prayer and praise of God, the two Ps not the two Ds. Prayer certainly served me well both during the fall of China and in Ireland during the war when I spent lonely nights by myself on the grounds of Magheramena Castle at Belleek. When I left in Spring 1946, the RUC gave me the nine-mm rifle that was programmed to assassinate me — there is a Guardian Angel.

In those early days during and after the war, drugs were not a problem in the U.S. Over much of the Far East, however, drug addiction was firmly instilled in the populations. Except for Japan, the poor, as well as some of the upper classes of the region, lived and died on brain transforming drugs.

In the rural regions it was mainly beetle nut, in the cities opium. The opium addicts were very easy to spot on the streets from the strange stare of their eyes — a sort of dilated "squint." They walked the streets of Shanghai, Canton and Bangkok in droves. During the "killing fifties" the Chinese communist leaders eliminated drugs (brought in by the colonial British to produce wealth) by slaughtering the drug addicts by the millions. The lonely are most often prey.

Strangely enough, on those lonely Irish nights I was extremely happy. I love people, but as Thomas Merton has pointed out (1) everyone needs time alone to think and pray. Late at night the wind whistling through the giant beech trees that lined the road to the castle, and the often present rain on the shingled barracks roof instilled a peaceful quietude conducive to study and prayer. I was in a candlelit GI monastery during those days of Irish bliss.

I read by candlelight on most nights since, after the war, the station went on standby, and cranking up the huge motor for two sixty-watt light bulbs was not worth the effort. I learned how Abraham Lincoln became serene by reading in candlelight.

As I lit the candle and placed it in front of my Nikon camera, my mind slowly drifted back to the little wooden insectary at Kansas State College. It sat near the edge of the dirt football field parking lot. Nearby were a few old Victorian houses and a small square plot of fertile soil. That plot produced my experimental corn, mostly hybrids, but it also contained a few scraggly inbred strains. The inbreds were more attractive to the corn earworm moth than hybrids. However, the greatest attraction to the night-flying corn earworm moth was the bluish mercury vapor streetlight which cast its glow on the insectary screening.

My Winnie and I moved to Manhattan, Kansas, into a small, on-campus apartment for veterans, which edged the practice football field. We left Fayetteville and the University of Arkansas, where I had finished two degrees. We loaded our two little daughters, Cathy and Margaret, Winnie's sewing machine, and my bird and bug books into our old V-8 Ford and drove to Kansas.

As is usual for students by the next summer we were out of money — my GI Bill ended. Winnie took a job on the inconvenient evening shift at the county hospital. Each evening I carried Cathy and Margaret, one under each arm, down to the insectary and then back to Winnie when she returned at midnight from the hospital.

Until they fell asleep on their blankets, they scrambled about the screened-in room catching my escaped corn earworms and returning them to their respective cubicles. They learned early the ways of science and scholarship. Cathy became a teacher and Margaret a landscape architect.

I, as might be expected of a moth lover, was observing the behavior of the corn earworm adult moths around candles, lightbulbs and cornplants. I soon found out that, contrary to popular belief, the moth eye has little to do with the insect's attraction to light. In fact, the fatal attraction lay in the two antennae located on the insect's head (2).

Those organs are unique structures covered with thousands of little spines called sensilla. My Ph.D. thesis was of a morphological nature, directed toward describing the complex reproduction, especially the hour-long copulation period, of noctuid moths. The male inserts what might be called a plastic sac (3) filled with sperm into the birth canal of the female. Each new mating leaves a new sac. Through dissection one can tell how often a Lepidoptera (butterfly or moth) has mated. I was the first ever to utilize this mating phenomenon to describe the mating percentages of any insect. The technique is of extreme value in plotting the destructive populations of night-flying moths. The one family of moths called Noctuidae is responsible for sixty to eighty percent of crop insect destruction in vegetable fields.

Although morphology was of extreme interest to me, the most intriguing aspect of those long nights in the insectary was my black box experiment that told me, in no uncertain terms, that moths are not attracted to candles or flickering light through their eyes, but rather to the air space around light. They are attracted by flickering scent molecules set to oscillating by the vibrating antenna and resonated, or tuned to by "pumping" the light from the night sky or from the ubiquitous mercury vapor streetlight. Entomologists used just such a blacklight (UV) fluorescent bulb with baffles sticking out around it to trap night-flying insects. It is called a blacklight trap.

After finishing my morphological studies of the moth reproductive tract, I began work on the antenna. This was much more difficult for each structure is covered with thou-

Moths at a candle. The candle flame emits hundreds of narrow-band, partially coherent (maser-like), infrared lines. Different species of insects are attracted to these coded lines (like bars on a cereal box). They mimic the scatter (coherent) emissions of thousands of different insect scents. The cabbage looper male is attracted to his death in a candle flame. One of the flame lines is a 17-micrometer infrared line that also comes from the female sex scent (pheromone). The candle is a true "femme fatale" to the male. The candle infrared lines are also healing lines, as sick elephants can attest.

Corn earworm moth (*Heliothis zea*) attracted to a plastic window with low-intensity light on it (0.87 foot candles). As long as there is no corn scent in the enclosed box, the moth does not fly into the blue beam and trigger his own photograph. Once corn scent is blown into the box, the moth flies to the lighted window. The low-intensity blue light stimulates the scent infrared emissions to a higher energy level and the little spines, called sensilla, act as fiber optic waveguides to further amplify the scent infrared frequencies.

sands of little spines called sensilla. They are the detectors (as was postulated then) for the scents to which the insects are attracted.

It took me almost fifteen years to produce my 108-page monograph on the moth antenna (4). It was the first detailed morphology of any insect antenna except for a few done on the very large moths in the Saturnidae family. These Saturnidae morphologies were not plotted in any detail or very well illustrated. It was during these nighttime observations that I noticed that the female vibrated her wings and extended her abdomen prior to mating. I knew scent was involved, and years later the scent was extracted by chemists.

The obvious plan was to design an experiment that could demonstrate that the insect needed both the environmental light and the scent for attraction to a mate or to a plant scent. In other words, the night sky light puts energy into the vibrating scent molecules causing the molecules to emit coded attraction frequencies in the infrared spectrum.

The mechanism was the same as that of the parking lot mercury vapor light. Those lamps are filled with molecules of mercury vapor. The electricity and photons from electrodes at either end stimulate the vapor to emit invisible UV light. In order to make the UV light visible, the glass tube is coated with a chemical called a phosphor that glows and visibly emits when irritated with the invisible UV light. It is the glow our eyes pick up. Like the insect antenna, our eyes also have little "sensilla" on the retina (detector). They are called rods and cones.

Insect antenna on one species or another have over 300 different shaped rods, cones, spines, pits and loops on them (5). Common sense alone would tell us that due to the very many shapes of these organs, the energy transfer from vibrating (oscillators) scents to the antenna is a frequency phenomenon. Only the morphologists seemed to understand what I was talking about. They believe that the shape of an organ probably means something. To this very minute as I write, not a single insect physiologist has ever answered my question, "What do the shapes mean?" One researcher went so far as to answer my question with the *non sequitur*, "They just evolved." The fact is, it does not matter to those who study scent that there are numerous different forms of sensilla on the insect antenna. I soon learned to feel sorry for their linear way of thinking, more to the point, their total ignorance of nature's subtle designs.

I spent the last few months of my Kansas State project building an oblong black box.

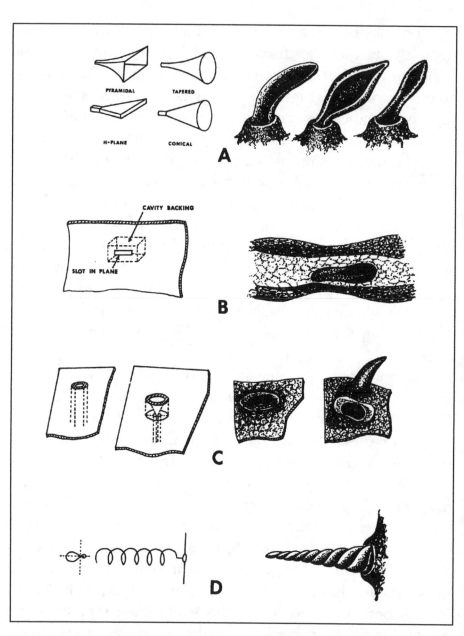

Comparison of man-made metal antenna (left) with insect waxy coated spine and cavity antennas. A. horn shape (shoehorn). B. long cavity shape. C. round cavity shape. D. helical or spine shape. Every one of the hundreds of man-made antenna shapes can be found on one insect species or another. Insect antennae really are antennae.

I reared enough corn earworms in my cubicle for several different tests with various colored lights. I felt with certainty that the night sky light of low-intensity blue, and UV light, of which there is plenty at the peak mating time (three to five a.m.), put energy into the attractive scents and caused them to resonate to the antenna spines.

In radio the ability of an antenna to "tune" to a frequency is similar to frequencies being fingered on a violin string — different wavelengths match the length of the strings. Insect antenna spines are of the length (dimensions) of tiny infrared wavelengths (micrometers long).

In one side of an enclosed black chamber (with a glass front) I placed a corn plant; on the other side was a circular hole with a cotton cloth stretched over it. Approximately 0.87 foot candles of blue light was projected through the cloth surface. Although the box contained more molecules around the outgassing corn plant than two feet away at the hairy surface, over 98% of the moth eggs were laid on the blue-irradiated cotton fibers instead of the corn plant's hairy silk. As I had postulated, the light scatter was stronger from the cotton fibers than from the corn plant. I found that the blue light raised the energy level of the corn scent molecules because the blue shone stronger on the cotton close to the lamp (6).

In later experiments I watched the behavior of moths at candles and light bulbs. They spiral in a log periodic fashion to a candle flame or around a light bulb; however, they are only attracted to a modulated (60 cycles per second, or hertz, flicker) light bulb with molecules of scent around it. In other words, attraction to electric light sources involves scent, light and flicker (modulation) — not light alone.

I read in the fields of antenna electrical engineering and physics. Early on I was struck by the elegant work on scatter radiation, especially from natural objects (7). That early

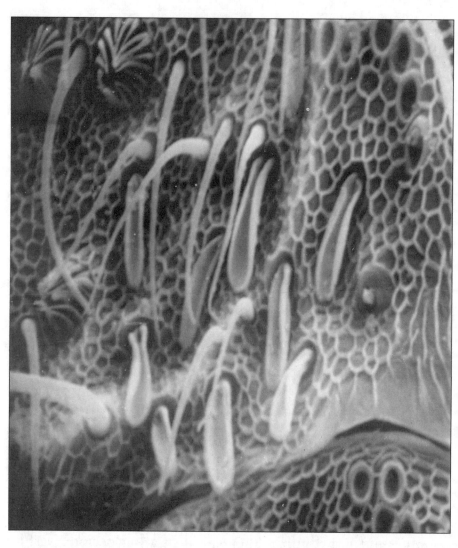

Antenna of moth, of a family of night fliers (unknown species). The corn earworm moth is a noctuid. They are the most common family containing over 2,000 species, 50 or 60 of which destroy agricultural crops. Healthy plants do not attract such insects as they do not emit the fermenting molecules of ammonia and ethanol that sick or old plants do. Insects are scavengers on plants that are sick or aged. They recycle organic matter. Plowing paramagnetic rock granules into dead soil will revive it. Note the three types of antenna: upper right — picket fence; middle — shoehorn; and spine. Note also the hexagon "etched" antenna scatter surface at the base of the spines. Molecules of scent hitting such a naturally designed surface scatter out as coherent (maser-like) radiation.

infrared emission work demonstrated that much of what physics calls "scatter" is actually not scatter, but coherent radiation. The fact that scatter from certain surfaces in nature is coherent (7) suggests that we might be able to design scatter systems to attract insects.

Almost any surface in nature must, someplace in the electromagnet spectrum, emit coherent scatter. This makes the field of surface morphology extremely important to any understanding of how nature operates, e.g., surface of skin, surface of a leaf, or the surface of a candle flame.

Not long after I left Kansas, we moved to Baton Rouge, Louisiana, where I joined the LSU Entomology Deptartment. At LSU I continued my nighttime light-scent studies under a National Science Foundation grant. During this time I refined my findings by flowing scent across a mirror with low-intensity light shining on it from a UV bluelight bulb. I soon found out that if I shook the scent by vibrating, either a spine (reed), or a mirror, in front of the low-intensity bulb, I could attract ten times as many moths as usual (see woodcut chapter heading). My findings were complete; scent molecules in nature were stimulated to emit energy by shaking them and causing collisions between the little oscillating balls of energy (called modulation). By blowing the scent through low-intensity blue UV light, and modulating them at the vibrating mirror at the same frequency as the moth vibrated its wing while flying (40 to 60 Hz), I could attract many, many more moths. In short, I had decoded olfaction, and discovered that it was not only electronic, but also photonics that worked the system. That is, it depended on the vibrating molecules losing an electron from their atom (electronics), and thus generating photons of infrared light which carried the message to the little spines on the antenna.

The findings were all published in both entomological journals (8) and *Applied Optics*, a physics journal. The papers excited the science world of scent and entomological research about as much as plastic jewelry would excite a debutante. Although this work was unaccepted by many, fortunately I was rewarded by my supervisors at the USDA in Tifton, Georgia, where I moved to a government position after leaving LSU. They saw to it that I was not only promoted, but I also received the Superior Service Award for my antenna frequency work (9).

With the USDA, I continued my insect antenna work for twenty more years in peace and quiet. Quiet is not only necessary for good research, it is also a part of thoughtful religious worship.

I have spent so much time in front of Mary and those beautiful votive candles that I eventually realized that the Christian religion does not always get across the main message of Christ's life. Christ's life demonstrated that loving original work — whether of charity, healing, or science — is seldom rewarded. Christ was the ultimate example of how evil (hypocrisy) ensures that the just are seldom rewarded, and are often crucified, as He was.

I soon learned that fame in science, or in any field, is a ridiculous want. For one thing, fame breeds a jealousy that quenches good research. I also learned that entomology is fun, and that study leads to thinking about other aspects of nature, such as rocks. In any case, my studies led me to thinking about the works of the great and gentle mathematician Einstein — and of the paradox he called curved time.

CHAPTER VIII
The Virgin and the Magpie

To me every hour of light and dark is a miracle
Every cubic inch of space a miracle.

Miracles
Walt Whitman

I finished my Ph.D. at Kansas State and moved to Louisiana State University in Baton Rouge to teach. After several years, I quit and went to work for the USDA. It was in my laboratory in Gainesville, Florida, that I received a call from Jody Smith that sent me on a journey to Mexico City.

From the window of the silver 727 I could see the pink glow of the falling twilight behind the mountains surrounding Mexico City. There were storm clouds and thunderous flashes of lightning illuminating the ground as we let down across the mountain pass called Rio Frio. I knew the mountain region well; years before I had camped across its length and breadth, trapping night-flying moths that flew to the eerie glow of my UV blacklight trap.

The pass was well named Rio Frio, for the nights were cold, and the solitude overwhelming among the ghostly pines that mantled the tree slopes.

I had great luck trapping the largest of the night-flying moths that inhabit the region. It is called the witch moth, and, like the mountain pass, it is well named. It is huge for a moth species, and is highly attracted to the infrared frequencies that the ultraviolet (blacklight) trap stimulates in the atmospheric molecules that surround the light.

As in the case of the infrared narrow lines emitted from scent molecules stimulated by visible and UV light, the candles also put out very narrow coherent (like radio) far infrared lines. All species of the moth family Noctuidae (owlet moths) are highly attracted to candles. The candle is the most powerful source of multiple, invisible, radio-like, infrared frequencies known to mankind. There are organic dye lasers that can be stimulated to put out a few visible "in tune" colors, but a burning candle emits hundreds upon hundreds of narrow coherent ("in jtune") infrared frequencies (infrared colors) (1). The moth antenna has spines (rods) which are tuned, like the rods on your TV antenna, to the infrared frequencies. It is the antenna that brings the moth to candles and light, and not their eyes.

In Asia human breath is called the "spirit of life," and a candle the "spirit of breath." Candles are used in Thailand and Burma to cure sick elephants. It is dangerous for an elephant with elephant flu to lie on the ground for a long time because it compresses the already congested lungs. The mahouts surround the sick elephant with hundreds of temple candles and chant. Within hours, the great beast stands up cured.

The giant witch moths which danced at my tent light candle those many years before, did indeed present a Macbethian scene. They would dive at the candle, envelope the flame with their huge grey wings, and snuff out the "spirit of breath." Eventually they would singe their wings and fall in a frenzied heap. The mere fact that so simple an object as a wax candle can cure an elephant, attract a moth, or lock a romantic couple in soulful bliss over the dining table, is proof enough to me of the wisdom of the Catholic church in not throwing out the ancient candle along with the ancient Latin in its zeal to modernize (2).

I always seem to dream onboard 727's and other such flying monsters. As we touched concrete, my drifting thoughts returned from boyhood days with falcons and magpies. The magpie is one of my favorite bird species. It is almost human in its bird behavior; social for most of the year, but a solitary nester that builds a huge stick nest with a stick thatched roof to protect the young from the elements. It is a happy, mischievous bird, and some individuals can be taught to speak (3).

Like my fondness for moths, my love of birds goes back to when I was twelve years of age when I took my first pet magpie from its squawking mother along Sand Creek west of

Denver. Since boyhood I have kept several pet magpies, and often painted watercolors of my pets.

My love of birds caused me to get a degree in ornithology, but somehow the scientific study of birds took the beauty and romance out of my feeling for feathered creatures. I found that the cold, calculating collection of data about the love and life histories of my feathered subjects totally destroyed the deep-seated pleasure that I took in their mere being. In short, I enjoyed them most when I was least concerned with meddling in their lives. Birds are part of my soul, and one does not like to scientifically study one's soul.

I was on my way to Mexico to begin an adventure concerning Mexico's most miraculous image of the Virgin of Guadalupe. The Virgin Mary must have been quite fond of birds, as birds figure very prominently in the story of her appearance to Juan Diego on Tepeyac Hill. Don Antonio Valeriano, who gives the earliest account of the apparition of the Virgin of Guadalupe in Mexico, wrote: "He [Juan Diego] heard singing from atop the hill. It was like the singing of various beautiful birds. At times the voices of the hillside wildness seemed to echo in response. Their singing, very soft and pleasing, surpassed that of the coyoltotl and tyinizezn and other lovely song birds."

I am certain the Blessed Virgin must have loved birds very much to have utilized them to lure Juan Diego to the top of Tepeyac Hill. She certainly would not have utilized my favorite pet, the magpie, for its raucous call can hardly be considered soft, much less beautiful. Besides, it is not a gentle bird, smart, but at times obnoxious, and downright sinful like humans. In addition, the species does not occur south of central New Mexico, which is very far to the north of Mexico City. My choice of birds, the mischievous, sometimes mean magpie, and the peregrine falcon, which kills and eats soft gentle birds, would certainly not be the choice of the gentle mother of Christ, or would they?

I am certain that Mary would have been far more aware of moths at candles and oil lamps than modern man, who, even in rural Mexico has electricity. It no doubt disturbed her to see those strange creatures commit suicide by "burning themselves at the stake."

As I picked up my heavy camera bag and passed through customs, I was hoping Jody Smith, who has asked me to come, would be at the airport to meet me. He speaks Spanish; I do not, despite the fact that my ancestors came from Mexico. My middle name, Serna, is a common name in Mexico City, where my great-grandmother on my mother's side grew to womanhood.

I was eager to inspect closely the famous image of Guadalupe. On my previous moth collecting trip to Mexico sponsored by the National Science Foundation, I stayed with friends who worked for the Rockefeller Foundation. When they drove me to the old basilica, the bishop happened to be speaking, and I could not get close as crowds filled the huge square. I had read about the Virgin of Guadalupe image, but did not know the details of how Christ's mother appeared to the Indian farmer Juan Diego on top of Tepeyac Hill, and asked him to have a church built there in her honor, or how the miraculous image appeared on his tilma cloak in front of the Franciscan Bishop in Mexico City.

I was able to view the image through the huge basilica doors, but could not get close enough to really appreciate its beauty. I soon forgot all about my less successful visit in 1957.

Jody did meet me at the gate. Jody, a Methodist and a native of Macon, Georgia, graduated from Emory Theological Seminary, and teaches philosophy at Pensacola State in Florida. He had visited the Basilica of Our Lady of Guadalupe, and was struck by the beauty of the Virgin's face. In idle conversation with Monsignor Salazar, the pastor of the basilica, he mentioned the work being done on the Shroud of Turin at that time. Father Salazar thought that perhaps a similar study could be accomplished on the Virgin of Guadalupe, but doubted that the Abbot (Bishop) would allow any such research. The image is difficult to get to as it was mounted behind bulletproof glass at the front of a huge steel vault in the back altar wall of the new Basilica. Besides, since the image had been carried on the battle flag of the Mexican revolution, it was considered both a church relic and a state treasure. Only the State Architect had a key to the vault, and the Director of the Mexican National Art Museum would also have to be present during any research, as well as church representatives and police officials (4).

As Jody described the difficulties of persuading conservative church and government officials to allow an unknown philosopher and an insect scientist to do research on their holy image, the whole idea seemed to border on the ludicrous.

I remember telling my wife that the Methodist preacher "was as crazy as a hoot owl." Hoot owls, of course, are not crazy, and as it turned out neither was Professor Jody Smith. Jody, by any standard, is a lovable and remarkable human being. It is true that at times his gruff and down to earth personality can grate on one, but then so did St. Peter on those who knew him best.

Jody Smith had seen me on the *Good Morning America* television program as I explained my work on insects and UFOs to co-host Sandy Hill. I had obtained a good correlation between spruce budworm infestations in national forests, and nighttime UFO reports. I showed, in my lab experiments, that it was quite easy to to light up an insect with the same air space voltage generated by storm fronts. The huge mile-long

The center portion of the beautiful fresco on the walls of the convent chapel on top of Tepeyac Hill in Mexico City. It shows a magpie, which is not found in Mexico, defending the Virgin Mary from Juan Diego. The Virgin stands on a rock, not on an angel as depicted in the real image. The angel, dress decorations, and sunburst have been added to the original, simple, inexplicable image.

swarms of spruce bud worms migrate on just such storm fronts. *Applied Optics*, the journal of the Optical Society of America, published my paper on insects as UFOs (5).

Thus it was a twist of fate (or was it?) that my insect migration studies were taking me, a bird lover and falconer, to Mexico City for a second time where I could view the beautiful image of the Virgin of Guadalupe. I had little hope that Jody and I would be allowed to do research on the image, but at least in the beautiful basilica I would be able to view the image from the moving pathway that takes pilgrims past the image behind the altar, regardless of mass before the altar. It is a very clever arrangement to allow the faithful from all over the world to view the Virgin of Guadalupe with no obstruction to the view. Mary must have a special place in her heart for the Mexican engineers who built the system.

Indeed people of many diverse faiths come to admire the beautiful image that hangs over the high altar of the great Basilica of Guadalupe. The modern basilica was built to house the image, and dedicated in 1976. The old basilica, a magnificent Spanish Romanesque structure has been slowly sinking into the soft lake bed of Mexico City. It has become so cracked and weakened that the Mexican Government closed its doors a few years ago for fear of a disaster. That the church still survives intact is a tribute to the Mexican faithful who built the ancient structure in 1709.

More remarkable even than the commitment of the Mexican builders of both the modern and ancient basilicas, is the long enduring belief that the sacred image appeared instantaneously on the cactus cloth (tilma) of a simple Indian farmer. When Juan Diego told the Bishop about his vision on Tepeyac Hill, the Bishop requested a sign from the Lady of Tepeyac Hill. Juan Diego returned, and Our Lady filled his tilma cloak with roses growing on the desert hilltop in

December. Juan Diego brought the flowers back to the Bishop, and as they dropped to the ground the beautiful image of the Virgin of Guadalupe was imprinted on the cloak. The image is a masterpiece as the face, so simply executed of almost "plaster-like" quality, is one of the most beautiful in the world. It makes the Mona Lisa look second rate.

Jody and I spent three days in Mexico City attempting to get permission to study the image. We were disheartened as our time was running out. Because of my research, I was due

One of the two magpies I painted for my mother (Christmas, 1951) is shown killing a snake. I have never seen a magpie kill a snake, nor does Jean M. Linsdale, in her detailed *The Natural History of Magpies*, list snakes as prey. This was artistic license, but very unscientific. The story of the Virgin of Guadalupe contains the biblicial prediction that Mary, representing womankind, will crush the serpent. One of the gods of Indian human sacrifice was, of course, the serpent god.

to return home on Sunday. Finally, we decided to stay one more day, and return Tuesday. The Monsignor had said he would meet with us one more time on Monday morning. There was nothing we could do on Sunday, so we went to Mass in the basilica, then walked to the little chapel on top of Tepeyac Hill.

In the 1940s an artist, I do not know who, painted a series of six frescoes of the incidents on Tepeyac Hill. They are beautifully executed, three on either side of the hilltop chapel.

Previous to viewing those frescoes, my own first viewing of the image of the Virgin of Guadalupe had not moved me as it did Jody Smith. I had seen, as D.H. Lawrence has written in his beautiful essay on New Mexico, "a hint of wild religion of the Indian sort" in the beautiful image. As Lawrence said, "I looked at their religiousness from the outside, for it is still harder to feel religion at will than to love at will."

As I walked through the wide doors of the little chapel on top of Tepeyac Hill, I glanced at a beautiful fresco to the right of the doorway.

There was a deep and sweeping sense of *déjà vu* that overwhelmed me at the moment I viewed this first of the six beautiful frescoes. Unbelievably, between the kneeling figure of Juan Diego and the vision of the Virgin, there was a magpie — a bird that does not migrate, and is a resident one thousand or more miles north of Mexico City.

In that fresco, which is located just to the right of the chapel doors, the magpie is in the tail up alert position and looking straight at Juan Diego, feet braced for battle, as if trying to guard the Virgin until it decides if Juan Diego is good or evil (6).

Of all the birds chosen for this painting, the magpie is most representative of mankind. In Colorado it was, until just lately, unprotected since it was considered a pest by ranchers.

In Ireland and England it is considered lucky or unlucky to see one depending on which legend one believes. A well-know legend relates that one of the reasons for the magpie's wickedness is because it is the only bird that refused go into the ark. The magpie has the reputation of being stubborn, as children often are, of being brave or good, bold or curious. In China, where it also occurs (it is a worldwide species in temperate zones), it is called Hy Tsia and thought of highly because its chatter warns the field hands of the presence of tigers. They are happy guardian birds, with over four-hundred vernacular names around the world. Here was one brave magpie guarding Our Lady of Tepeyac Hill.

There is no evidence that magpies kill snakes. They are insectivores, and thus beneficial to agriculture. Yet in 1951, I painted a pair for my mother showing one killing a snake. Why? I do not know, but it is a very unscientific painting since no bird book or treatise on magpies lists snakes as prey.

The snake has always been associated with the Virgin of Guadalupe as an Indian symbol (serpent god). It is said that Juan Diego's uncle, Juan Bernardino, was very sick, and was cured when he too had a vision of the Virgin Mary. He told his nephew that the precious image would crush the serpent.

In 1951, when I painted the picture, I had never been to Mexico City. I had not the slightest notion about anything concerning the image much less the snake story, yet the painting I gave my mother depicts a magpie crushing a serpent.

On that day, my mind became jumbled with thoughts of the strange coincidences that led to my standing before this fresco. Was it my love of birds, or was it the *Good Morning America* television program where Jody Smith had learned I was a world authority on the use of infrared radiation, that brought me to Mexico City?

It was most certainly my UFO migration study, otherwise Jody would never have come to know me. How about my love of moths and candles? Without that passion, I would not have spent my life studying the infrared portion of the spectrum. For thousands of years candles have been burned in Catholic churches in honor of Mary.

What of insects? I recall a saying by Mary Howitt, "He is happiest who has power to gather wisdom from a flower." I was always happiest gathering wisdom from insects. "Find God in little things," as the hymn so peacefully proclaims.

My next startling discovery at that fresco was indeed a "little thing."

I could barely see the painted figure in the dim light of the chapel. In the background, behind the kneeling figure of Juan Diego, was a conquistador. I could not believe that on his fist was a falcon. I pressed my face tightly against the protective bar in front of the fresco. On the gloved fist of the Spanish soldier was a falcon raised towards heaven. Ahead of the conquistador was an Indian hunter with a spear, obviously a servant of the Spaniard.

I have a library of more than forty rare books on the art and practice of falconry, and, although falconry was practiced until the 17th century in Spain, there was not a single piece of evidence that the conquistadors brought the sport to Mexico. This simple fact is often commented on in books on the subject (7).

I put my telephoto lens through the iron bars and clicked a photo of the little falconer. I wanted to make sure when I got home that it was indeed a falconer, and that my mind was not making my eyes see something that wasn't there.

Jody walked up to me as I turned toward him, and I said, "Jody, tomorrow the authorities will let us do our infrared study of the image. My life is in that fresco."

The cover watercolor for my 1981 monograph on the image of the Virgin of Guadalupe. On the right is the painting as it is now viewed, with blue mantle, stars, decorations and sunburst painted over the original. A is a simple sketch of a drawing as it would have been seen if one were drawn under the image — there is no drawing. B is the background drawn on by man. Infrared also shows the original (C & D) as an Indian maiden standing on a rock. The shadow of the pink robe resembles the shadow of an agave plant. Agave is the cactus (century plant) cloth on which the image is painted. On the left (C&D) is the representation of the single plain pink and blue mantle and face of the Virgin. Since I found iron oxide and copper sulphate in the basalt-type rock of Tepeyac Hill, and also some white limestone, I am assuming that those soil pigments were drawn to the waxy surface of the cloth tilma by a process known as electret photography. It is simple in the lab to produce such an image.

"I have the same feeling," Jody replied as we walked out the chapel doors.

The next evening at six p.m., after the last basilica mass, the very conservative Mexican Catholic church and, even more, the very conservative Mexican government, spent two hours taking the sacred image from behind the beautiful bulletproof and metal frame and setting it inside the vault.

The Abbot, Director of the National Art Museum, and three high-ranking police officials spent the entire night with Jody and myself in the vault. The Director of the Art Museum making quite sure I knew what I was doing with their miraculous masterpiece. We were the first scientists in over 200 years allowed such privileges. That was a miracle in itself.

I found, with the infrared film, that there was no drawing under the image, and that the face turned olive color from a distance, not from pigment, but from diffraction light (an impossibility for an artist). The original blue mantle and robe of pinkish color were uncracked, and as bright and new as the image would have been in 1530 when it happened. All the paint that was cracking off had been added centuries later, probably to cover dirt from the millions of faithful that in early centuries touched and handled it. It was, in short, a rose and blue pigmented Shroud of Turin. The pigments appeared to be blue copper sulfate from soil, and iron oxide also from the soil. The iron oxide was impregnated with the tilma plant layer of wax to give it a rose-colored hue.

One can definitely prove an object to be inexplicable by present day scientific methods. The image of the Virgin of Guadalupe is inexplicable.

Over the past few years, I have received a lot of letters putting forth the writers' views about my infrared investigation of the image of the Virgin of Guadalupe in Mexico City. Some of these writers take exception to my findings that, although

Closeup of the detail of the protecting magpie. Bottom, small background figure of a Spanish falconer. The hunting bird can be seen on the fist of the horse-man conquistador. The upper photo also shows a wren. For twenty-seven years the wren has nested in our backyard. This fresco depicts my life as a naturalist (see Part I). Materialists will call it a coincidence. I call it Divine Providence.

the original image is inexplicable, the Spanish Gothic decoration on and around it have been added by human artists. Others comment in great detail that, even if my work is scientifically accurate, I missed the whole point since I am neither an artist nor a theologian, and have been misled by my infrared photographs. Still others point out that my work is rather nice, but it is the computer-enhancement research on the reflection of Juan Diego in the image eye that really proves the image is miraculous. In good faith, I could not take exception to what any of these writers say, and certainly delight in my critics' letters. What is curious about some of the letters is the mysterious and somewhat disconcerting feeling that I get that the writers believe that my motives for the study were neither appropriate nor scientific. They believe miracles should not be investigated, only believed by the faithful. The other side of the coin is that I tarnished my reputation as a scientist by even believing that such religious superstitions are worthy of study.

When my mother died many years ago, I found this note and poem among her papers. She obviously, in her quiet manner, approved of my work.

Dearest Phil:
Your great grandmother was Eloisa Serna, daughter of a wealthy Mexico businessman. She was married in a society wedding in Mexico City to Manual D'Ainsa.

There are thoughts too deep for words as it should be.
There are pains as deep as swords which none can see,
But there is heaven, with all fulfilled forever more
When Angels pass and lift us to that Golden door.

My work in Mexico City led me to believe that many mystical happenings will eventually be explained by science. St. Augustine has written that miracles are temporal, that is, worldly. In short, since God created nature, He can easily manipulate it to send us special communication called "miracles." Such signs are, after all, messages from God. Since Jesus is God, and lived in this world, He most probably knows enough of His own masterwork, nature, to utilize it to communicate with we less than Godly mortals. In other words, "miracles" are not supernatural because they contradict nature, but because God commands His elegant field of physics to stimulate a sacred miracle .

I will never really know why all this happened to me. I only know for certain that there are indeed thoughts too deep for wonder, and pain aplenty as my mother wrote. I also know, for myself at least, that an angel passed and lifted me through the golden doors of the Basilica of the Virgin of Guadalupe. My life was changed forever, and for that I thank my good friend Jody Smith and the Mother of God. As a scientist, an insect migration expert, a candle and magpie lover, and a falconer, I did my best (8).

CHAPTER IX
Divine Providence

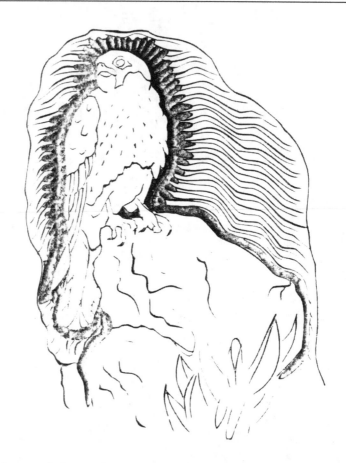

Then we believe what we cannot see and we hope for what we can only imagine. Oh! how we are brought to perfection by this hidden activity of which we are both the subject and the instrument, though we know nothing of it, for all we do seems to be the result of pure chance and our natural inclinations.

Abandonment to Divine Providence
Jean-Pierre DeCaussade

Life goes forward from incident to incident (in space). I write, as do most authors, in a sequence of time from the incidents in boyhood concerning falconry and magpies, to my travels as I wandered from the United States to Ireland, and around the world (in Part I; Part II is different).

Once in a while life tells us that time is not a straight line, but that out there, where God is (the spirit world), time can go + or -, backwards or forwards.

Long before I arrived in Mexico, God had seen to it that someone placed my boyhood life on a chapel wall. Life is like that where God is concerned, but so is our memory.

We can place incidents anywhere we want in time. Memory goes back and imagination goes forward. It is indication of a time shift that although I went to Mexico to study the Virgin of Guadalupe in 1979, I went to Le Puy (as described in this chapter) long before that trip, on my way to the 1960 International Congress of Entomology. In my memory, for some strange reason Guadalupe seems always to have occurred before Le Puy.

In other words, my imagination goes backward to Guadalupe then turns around and comes forward to Le Puy. Perhaps this is because God, through Mary, wants me to remember it that way. "The first shall be last and last first." Memory is never linear (straight line), but rather it is nonlinear (crooked), as is time.

If messages (or incidents) could really go forward or backward in time, scientists would call the photons carrying such messages tachyons, or particles of energy faster than the fixed speed of light at 300,000 km per second.

Our imagination works like tachyons. It goes backward and forwards, but only concerning things in the past. It cannot go into the future (unless, of course, one is a prophet).

Perhaps I think forward to Le Puy, which happened in the past before Guadalupe, because it was at Le Puy that I first noticed what the rest of this book is about, and what I have discovered of the soil — a force called paramagnetism. I first came across that force in Le Puy. I have also lately discovered that time is really *timespace* (Einstein), and can indeed go up and down, or backwards and forwards as *waves of time* (see appendix).

The mountain town of Le Puy is not on any regular tourist route. It perches at the edge of the Massif Central, isolated from the main thoroughfares of France. The Massive Central is the mountainous black rock plateau of central France. Many great Frenchmen have been conceived and raised to manhood in the volcanic cup of rock, Teilhard de

Le Puy as a place of pilgrimage predates all the 19th- and 20th-century sites by over a thousand years. It is known that the town has been renowned as an apparition site since the middle of the 9th century. The first crusade, begun by Peter the Hermit, started from Le Puy. Thirteen kings of France, and a whole line of popes beginning with Urban II, visited the site. Charlemagne is said to have visited, as did Joan of Arc's mother in 1429. The Holy image in the Moorish looking Cathedral is known as the Black Virgin, and is believed to be given to the people of Le Puy by Saint-Louis the King. On the right side is the large Romanesque Arab (Mideastern-type) appearing Cathedral of Le Puy; to the far left St. Michael D'Aiguilha on its basalt needle.

Chardin being one of the best known. Teilhard, that indefatigable philosopher-priest, must have absorbed much of his mystic energy from the black basalt of the region.

Maurice Barrie has written of the town Le Puy (the needle) that in his opinion it is: "The most attractive, the most

Lourdes — View from the mountainside of the beautiful Basilica of the Immaculate Conception. Under the large, grassy lawn is the huge underground Basilica of St. Pius X, where thousands can attend mass. The grotto where the Virgin Mary appeared to St. Bernadette on Feb. 11, 1858, is at the right side and at the rock base of the Basilica. St. Bernadette, a little shepherd girl, and daughter of a poor couple living in a deserted jail house in Lourdes, went with two friends to collect wood for their fireplaces. She waded across the little stream that flowed in front of a rocky cliff where a hollow grotto had eroded into the cliff. The grotto was the the dumping spot for the filthy output of the local hospital. The Virgin appeared to Bernadette on a rocky ledge above a garbage dump — a dump no longer except for the troubles of the faithful left behind at the rocky grotto.

strange, and indeed rarest of all of French towns." I agree. Its attractiveness, if not its strangeness, may center in a huge high cone of black basalt rock situated in its very center. The stone and brick dwellings that climb the sides of the cone stop at a rocky, flat top. In the center of the rock peak is a four-story-high statue of the Virgin and Child. It is one of the little-known masterpieces of central Europe. The gentle eyes of Mary and Child sweep over the surrounding fertile farmland.

I had first learned of Le Puy as I had first learned of Falconry, in the pages of an old *National Geographic* magazine.

The sick attended by volunteers called handmaids, one for each pilgrim. Over 50,000 desperately ill faithful are brought to Lourdes each year. There have been thousands of healings, although only 64 have been well documented by scientists up through 1978. These are the ones considered by the church to be absolutely miraculous. The sick in this photograph are seen leaving the lower Basilica of the Rosary after mass.

I did not plan to visit Le Puy. I hardly had time to visit Paris and Chartres with its famous cathedral of Mary. I was due in Vienna for the International Congress of Entomology. Le Puy, I decided, was too far off the beaten path.

I had spent a few hours absorbing the beauty of Chartres, and was leaving for the train station when I began a conversation, in the usual friendly tourist fashion, with an Episcopalian priest and his wife.

I had barely finished my speech about Le Puy being an even more "Mary" town than Chartres, when Divine

The faithful in front of the grotto where the Virgin appeared 18 times between Feb. 11, 1858 and July 16, 1859. On March 25, "the Lady," as Bernadette called her, revealed that she wished to be called the Immaculate Conception, meaning born without the original sin of Adam and Eve on her soul. It is evident from this photo that Lourdes, like Ireland, is a very rainy place because of its location in the French Pyrenees.

Divine Providence 115

The great statue of the Virgin and Child. In the foreground is Msgr. de Morlhon, Bishop of Le Puy, under whose direction the beautiful statue was erected. On July 28, 1860, the separate plates of the statue arrived in Le Puy from Givors where they were cast. It is one of the largest statues in the world, measuring, including the pedestal, over 74 feet tall. One can climb to the crown for a view of Le Puy.

Providence intervened. The priest and his wife had just rented a car, and were wondering where they should begin their visit to southern France. Before I knew it, I was in the back seat of the car heading directly for Le Puy, a six-hour drive. After leaving my friends, I climbed the central volcanic rock to the base of the great statue. The beautiful figure was accomplished by a young sculptor called Bonnassieux. A native of Loir, he won the commission from among fifty better-known artists. To cast the great statue, Napoleon III had donated the Russian cannons captured at the siege of Sabastopol. An ironmonger was commissioned to melt the cannons, and pour the red-orange liquid into the sculptured clay molds. On July 28, 1860, the great metal plates were dragged on wheels from Givors to Le Puy. On the dedication day, it was reported, over 100,000 people took part in the festivities presided over by Cardinal Donnet, Archbishop of Bordeaux (1).

History has it that in the first century of the church the Virgin Mary revealed herself on that black-rock slope of the Roche Corneille.

To this day, at the main entrance of the Moorish-looking Cathedral there is a megalithic block of black basalt called the "stone of fevers" (2). Mary and healing go together at every single one of her apparition rocks (3). I say rocks as almost every one of the geological locations of church-documented apparitions is a rock environ — Kerrytown in Ireland, Medjugorje, Guadalupe, La Salette, Lourdes, Le Puy, etc. The one exception is Knock, Ireland, which, although not a rocky terrain, is at least the rocky side of a stone church.

After leaving the base of the great statue, I climbed down the sides of the Roche Corneille and crossed the many lush vegetable gardens surrounding another, even steeper, sharp black cone of basalt. On the rock summit is a small, wonderfully formed chapel. It is so well matched to the basalt rock that it blends in as if invisible.

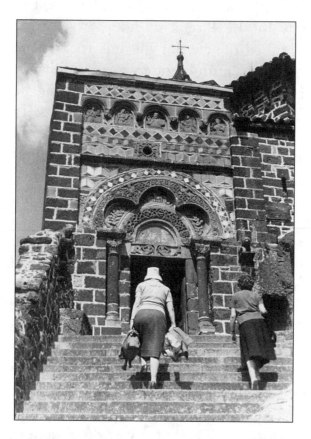

St. Michael D'Aiguilhe. In my opinion, this is one of the most beautiful small chapels in the entire world. The rock basalt pyramid, on which it perches like a winged angel, is 290 feet high and has a diameter at the base of 188 feet. Some 268 steps lead to the marvelous Romanesque Moorish facade It is an architectural masterpiece. At the top of the door God looks down surrounded by four angels. The rest of the facade is an intricate mixture of black basalt, red sandstone, and limestone blocks and triangles. In early times, the inside of the chapel was decorated all over with frescoes. Those on the vaulted roof still exist. It was at this spot, in 1960, that I began my search for the energy in stone that stimulates growth. By 1968, I had come to realize that it was the force called by John Tyndall *paramagnetism.*

Jean Romeau has written:

Nowhere undoubtedly does there exist such an unbelievable rock as that of Aiguilhe; it is exactly like a black and red sugarloaf on whose summit the enraptured people of the Middle Ages built an oratory, so perfect a monument that its steep stone-steeple seems to continue the steepness of the rock. Art and nature seem to have vied with each other to turn this unusual peak into one of the most characteristic beauties of Velay. This irregular pyramid is 290 feet high, and its diameter at the base measures 188 feet. You reach the top by a stairway of 268 steps cut into rock. This natural obelisk is dedicated to all the angels and especially Sts. Gabriel and Michael. The rock is wholly dedicated to angels, according to an old chronicler. St. Michael, however, is its master patron.(4)

It was at this rock of the angels that I first began my journey of research into a weak force in soil that operates to stimulate efficient plant growth. Crossing the vegetable gardens of Le Puy, I noted that they were totally free of disease and insect damage, and that almost all of the lushest ones surrounded the rocky base of the Chapel St. Michael D'Aiguilhe. They appeared to be planted in a manner to absorb whatever energy St. Michael radiated into their roots (5).

I climbed the stairs to the marvelous little jewel of architecture and spent, as I remember that day, at least one hour meditating before the altar. As I was leaving to descend the stairs, a small kestrel flew out from a rocky ledge of D'Aiguilhe. I sat on the stair wall at the entrance and watched it as it glided out over the green vegetable patches below — it was a green of such a hue as to be characterized as brilliant.

I crossed the gardens and worked my way up another hill in order to record on film the chapel rock and surrounding vegetable gardens. Unfortunately, my camera was loaded with black-and-white film instead of color. The kestrel dropped on a grasshopper in the green patch — God's bug catcher.

As I sat at dusk watching the sun set beyond Le Puy, my mind drifted back to my father's funeral many years before. He converted to the Catholic religion a week before his death. At his funeral, at the Fort Bliss Military Cemetery in El Paso, a desert kestrel flew out over the grave site. It happened just as the last volley of the military salute was given. At almost every major event of my life a kestrel appears. Like the magpies, the falcon has become a sign from God. It told me that everything was OK with my father — God would care for him. My thoughts about that military funeral brought back to me the anger and tears on my little sister Annie's face on the day after our father died in the Catholic hospital where a bishop resided. It was the Bishop who converted and baptized him the previous week. We went to the local parish priest who originally headed a seminary. This priest informed us that the bishop was senile, and so our father was not really baptized. He therefore could not be buried in a Catholic cemetery. I was angry, but one of the defects of my character is that after a short time my brain switches to sorrow for such misguided souls. One should pray for help in such a situation.

In my youth, shortly before the war, I drove to work at Normoyle Ordinance Motor Base in San Antonio with my father (6). During one conversation in the car, that I remember to this day, he advised me that at times life was like a battle and to remember, "Never, never go over anything you can go around."

The worst part of the incident was not the cemetery, but the fact that the priest would not say a mass in the local church for our father. Theologians say that murder, adultry, theft, etc. are mortal sins. I am no theologian, but I would guess, and most priests would agree, that refusing to say a mass for a deceased baptized soul is surely a mortal sin, as it involves both pride and unjust judgement — Pontius Pilate is the great example.

Remembering my father's words of wisdom, I decided to go around the misguided monsignor. Why not bury Dad in a military funeral and mass? Since my parents had married while stationed at Fort Bliss, I called my Uncle Frank in El Paso. My father was buried at Fort Bliss in a beautiful ceremony that included a military honor band and a mass.

One of my favorite persons, Frank, an attorney, handled his sister's estates. He is a generous uncle, with a kind and gentle heart. He is a master photographer, and was responsible for starting me on my journey as a competent photographer — one might say that his encouragement led to my life of experimentation with film and lens. It also pointed me toward the study of physics. I joined the Optical Society of America and published many of my papers in *Applied Optics*, a marvelous scientific journal edited by Dr. John Howard, Chief of Cambridge Air Force Research Lab.

Why did my father die in a Catholic hospital? To put it as succintly as I know how, because he was thrown out of one of the large Army-Navy Hospitals in the South, located in Hot Springs, Arkansas. He had retired there on military retirement pay, so he and my mother, who was in poor health, could receive good medical care.

The hospital was closed because the Republican Party decided to build a similar one in Kansas, due to the rather strange phenomenon called partisan politics, but I prefer to thank God for that true life phenomenon, Divine Providence. Although I am a Democrat, and a backer of government aid for the unfortunate, I do thank the Republicans for driving my father into the arms of God.

Incidents such as the above can easily lead to self pity, bitterness and a dropping out of religion. Blaming the misdeeds of one minister, rabbi, or priest on the encompassing ethics of a religion is to put one into the realm of dissatisfaction with God — a dangerous response to a very human misdeed by one other person.

As I walked back to my hotel room in Le Puy, I began to wonder what powerful force lay within rock. This force, at least to me, seemed to be involved in apparitions of God's mother, Mary.

After the meeting in Vienna I returned home. In my office at Louisiana State University, I took down my physics handbook and opened it. What caught my eye was *paramagnetism* and *diamagnetism*. Could this be it?

Had Divine Providence led me to Le Puy, and my father to the Christian religion when he was at death's doorway? Where would it take me if I had the sense to listen to God's whispers? In Egypt I was to find out.

CHAPTER X
Paintbox Explorer

Everyone has a source of creativity. It can be expressed in innumerable ways, depending on the unique experience of that person. Disbelief in the validity of personal experience and expression is the stumbling block for many artists, particularly as they measure themselves against the work and ideas of others. They hesitate to examine what they as individuals have to offer as something of real worth.

Watermedia — Techniques for
Releasing the Creative Spirit
Marilyn Hughey Phillis

I opened the book. As with all well thumbed books it opened, not by chance, at my favorite pages — birds of prey. It is a very large book called *Birds of America*, and was edited by T. Gilbert Pearson. I believe it has been reprinted a few times since I found it under the Christmas tree in 1939, a very few months after the invasion of Poland.

At the age of sixteen I had few thoughts of war, and no idea whatever that by age eighteen I would be up to my proverbial neck in it. The most thumbed page of all bore a description of the Cooper's hawk. In one column was a photograph of the eyas in a large stick nest. I had first seen the book in a department store in Detroit, and my mother, with a mother's instinct had, when we could ill afford it, paid $3.00 for the slick paper, fully colored and illustrated volume. Today it would sell for $40.00 or more.

I call it my nostalgia book because whenever I want to recall my wonderful boyhood, I will pull it off the shelf. One of the marvels of the human brain is that it can live comfortably in the present while going both backwards and forwards in time. Though we should live to the utmost in the present, we should never forget the past or not plan for the future.

I learned how to paint with watercolors by copying the beautiful paintings of Louis Agassiz Fuertes in *Birds of America*. Fuertes was tragically killed in 1927 when a train hit his car near his home in Ithaca, New York. Roger Tory Peterson, of bird field guide fame, followed him as a bird painter. I had no great artist as an inspiration living nearby, so learned all on my own. My reader may judge how well from my block cuts.

It is painting, especially with watercolors, that teaches one regard for detail. Both Fuertes and Peterson are honored for the fine detail of their feathered friends. As in science, detail in painting leads to discovery.

Sometime in my travels through life, I began reducing the rolls of film I shot during my adventures from ten or fifteen to one or two. For film I substituted four-by-six-inch blocks of watercolor paper and a pocket-sized paint set. For years I have carried it, with my small field glasses, a little millivolt meter (for measuring atmospheric voltage), and a small, hand-carved statue of Mary, in a camera case. I call it my explorer's kit as I carry it on every adventure. If I should lose my luggage or coat, fine; but the loss of my explorer's kit would be a disaster (1).

It does not take me long to find out that one does not need to pose a model, whether bird, insect, or human, in order to paint a good likeness. Furthermore, I believe that everyone has a photographic memory for life forms — they just never develop it.

Robert Henri had written in his book, *The Art Spirit*: "The most vital thing in the look of a face or of a landscape endure only for a moment. Work should be done from memory. The *memory* is the vital movement." I have never read such advice in any other art book!

Henri was, without a doubt, not only a competent artist, but America's greatest teacher of art. His little work is a classic of art literature, and he is a little known great man.

Carrying my watercolors around the world, I not only painted people, scenes and wildlife, but I observed them in far greater detail than I would have with a camera. I noted how cacti grew from solid rock cliffs, and how tree roots moved towards huge granite boulders. The questions I asked were no different than the ones that the so-called "new age" youth (whatever that means) of the '70s were asking.

What energy really emits from different kinds of rock? Why do I like to sit by certain trees? Why does an Indian hug a tree for a few hours on her honeymoon night? What do the leaves of a quaking aspen tree tell us?

In many cases the young people of the '60s and '70s, who were well meaning and of a poetic nature, received the answers by what the scientist would call insight and what the religious call visions. In many cases, however, they felt their visions should be amplified by chemicals, so they scrambled good insights with meaningless drug-induced thoughts. As is usual to such perverted things, anger and violence often ensues.

For those who avoided drugs and depended on their rather "homey" sort of praying, their insights were, as often as not, as valid as those obtained by me through experimentation. They knew for certain that a weak sort of resonant force exists in rocks and trees — they just did not have the experimental background to prove it.

For some strange and unbelievable reason I did learn, through a long series of happenings that I can only credit to Divine Providence, what these forces are and how to apply them to agriculture (2).

It was this knowledge that led me to Cairo, Egypt a few years back. I was invited there by a group of college professors to explain the work I conducted on soil and on the paramagnetic force (3). I ended my talk with a few words about the Aswan Dam. I was speaking in the great hall in Cairo. There was, when I finished, to repeat a literary cliché, a "deadly silence."

Over the past forty years I have come to regard insecticides and weed killers as the most destructive technology ever invented. Cigarettes only kill smokers, including my father who rolled (like a cowboy) three packs a day, and died at sixty-three of heart trouble. These despicable agricultural chemicals, however, kill the soil and indirectly effect every organism on the earth's surface.

Fat is a biological storage mechanism. Like soil, fat stores every poison invented by modern man in great quantities. It is well known that fat people store more environmental garbage than thin, and have a higher incident of cancer. Womens' breasts are a fat-storage mechanism — need I say more about breast cancer? Like the cigarette companies, the CEOs of large chemical corporations lie daily about the benefits of a form of chemical farming that is slowly destroying the world by man-made pollution.

To make it even worse, they foster forced growth with a leftover from World War II called anhydrous ammonia. That nitrogen-carrying chemical was used to make explosives for war. In order to keep the factories going, chemical companies foisted anhydrous ammonia off on the farmers of America.

In World War II, anhydrous ammonia was poured on the cow pastures of England to harden them (soil compaction) for landing fields.

Not only does the molecule compact the soil, but it is also the primary attractant for swarms of insects. One micro drop of it added to an insect attractant chemical will amplify the infrared attraction frequency lines three to ten times — in short, it makes sick plants (grown on poisoned soil), which out-gas excessive ammonia and ethanol (fermentation), even more attractant to scavenger insects (4).

It was my devotion to the mother of God, Mary, that led me to begin testing soil all over the world for a force that the physics handbook calls paramagnetism. I started these studies of this magnetic force by measuring the soil and rock at Mary's apparition sites. I have learned that at all such sacred places, Catholic as well as ancient, the force was extremely high. It was also high in the King's Chamber of the Great Pyramid at Giza.

At the conclusion of my talk in Cairo, I pointed out that the Aswan Dam blocked the yearly flooding of the Great Nile Valley. The White Nile brings organic matter from the western interior of Africa, and the Blue Nile brings paramagnetic eroded rock from the volcanic mountains of Ethiopia to the east. They join at Khartoum and fertilize the Nile valley at flood time. For forty years or so, the good earth has silted up behind the dam, and the Egypt that once exported food and cotton now imports 40% of its agricultural produce (5).

My suggestion was to move all people out of the river valley, and blow up the dam. After what seemed about two years (time is relative as I shall prove), a gentleman stood up and said, "Dr. Callahan you are absolutely right, and that is exactly what we should do!"

His words were no sooner out when my heretical speech received a standing ovation. As best as I remember, the only one I ever received. Heretics are not usually applauded — sitting much less standing.

That night as my wife and I mixed with the scientists and guests at the final reception, I inquired as to who the gentleman was. My professor friend smiled and replied, "Why that is Dr. Saaid, the vice-president of Egypt." The reason for the "deadly silence," and relieving ovation, was immediately apparent.

Prior to the meeting, my wife and I had spent several days measuring the paramagnetic value of Egyptian pyramid chambers (that are usually made of pink granite), and other Egyptian monuments constructed of granite.

The concept of paramagnetism is quite simple. A paramagnetic substance, mostly volcanic rock, goes toward a magnet; a diamagnetic substance, such as plant material, is pushed away from a magnet. I measured the force by hanging a rock, or soil in a glass tube, from a thread and measuring how far it went toward or away from a strong magnet (toward = paramagnetic; from = diamagnetic) (6). Grade 1 would be poor, not moving far in millimeters; grade 5 = excellent; and grades 2, 3, and 4 are in between. Almost every ancient structure, pyramid, megalithic tomb, Irish round tower, standing stone, as well as the rocks or soil around Mary's apparition sites, measured 4 (superior) to 5 (excellent).

Another phenomenon I have continued to observed, as I did in Le Puy, is that at such places the crops were growing in

Pink granite rock at Kerrytown, Ireland. In February, 1939, the Virgin Mary appeared on the rock (over a month long period) to 15 farmers and the parish priest. In May 1966, I interviewed Theresa (Ward) Boyle, who first saw the apparition when she was 15. She told me the spot where I have an arrow is where the Virgin first appeared. As is usual the local bishop ignored the words of honest people and the parish priest, and never attempted to investigate the apparition. Irish faithful still make pilgrimages to Kerrytown. The Rosses, as the area is known, is a wild and rocky region on the northwest coast of County Donegal. At this apparition site Mary said nothing, only pointed out to sea. Not long after the Virgin appeared, American and British ships began to be sunk by the German submarines a few miles out from the shore.

highly paramagnetic soil, with little or no insect damage. Experimenting with model structures, I found out that it was the paramagnetic force that controlled growth. I wrote a book on the subject called *Paramagetism — Rediscovering Nature's Secret Force of Growth.*

I titled it "rediscovering" because it was quite obvious that every ancient stone structure was designed to take advantage of this mysterious antenna force. I call it an antenna force, for such rocks and soil collect the magnetic fields of the earth and cosmos, temporarily store the energy, and throw it back into the roots of the oppositely charged diamagnetic plants.

I eventually discovered that agriculture flourishes in places where the earth is highly paramagnetic, and where it is weak chemical fertilizers and insecticides are needed. The plants are, to put it as strongly as possible, sick, and also are out-gassing ammonia and ethanol long before old age. Crops should never get old enought to be scavenged by insects because they are presumably harvested in their healthy youth.

Healthy plants grown in a highly paramagnetic soil do not attract insects. Insects are God's scavengers utilized to recycle old material.

As I traveled around the world with my paintbox and millivolt meter, I soon learned that, in the atmosphere above such highly paramagnetic soil and rock, the natural atmospheric frequencies generated by lightning (called Schumann frequencies for the German researcher who discovered them) were also much stronger. These were the places where the image of the Virgin Mary, more often than not, appears. Strangely enough, I also began to get a series of mystical photographs with Kodacolor and Fujicolor film.

In Medugorje, I photographed five narrow beams of "laser" lines coming from the dark steeple window at 5:45 p.m., the exact time the visionaries were observing Mary (7).

Farmhouse where the Ward family, father, mother, son, and two daughters, had visions of Mary outside their doorway at "the rock" (as it is still called). At this spot, the priest hunters of Cromwell's time slaughtered five Franciscan fathers. The statue with rosaries sits on a windowsill looking towards the "rock." The faithful who care for Kerrytown and the Ward's house have little money to keep the cottage in good shape. This photo was taken about 15 years ago and was my first "miraculous" photo. I took it in bright sunlight with the sun to my back standing directly in front of the statue. Note the tree reflected in the window. I leave it to my reader to figure out why this photo contradicts the physics of light reflection.

At Fatima it was several narrow "laser" lines down the front of the house where the little shepherdess, Lucia Santos, lived. I also obtained a cloud-like, ghostly form of an angel and the three visionary children at the first rocky apparition site.

There is also a photo of myself, taken on the wilds of the Huagramona river in the Amazon of Peru, with a huge red aura around my upper body. All of these photographs (like hundreds of others obtained by pilgrims of all Christain faiths) are taken on color films. Such films are made of the layered dyes of three primary colors. There is no way to fake these photographs, and the negatives are readily available for examination. The skeptical magician type will, of course, believe that I faked them.

Like my favorite image of a thinker, the Scarecrow of Oz, my brain worked diligently on the how and why of such obvious signals from God.

Like the Scarecrow, a magic character, I soon began to realize that real life is as mystical and magical as any land of Oz. God has seen to that.

Once many years ago, Jack Perkins, the famous correspondent, asked me if I, a well-known scientist, really believed in miracles. My answer was "Jack, do you believe in life?" He never answered, and NBC news ended the program with my question. Life, of course, is a miracle!

One more episode of Divine Providence was to enter my life on that Egyptian trip.

At the reception, the secretary of agriculture invited my wife and I to stay over one more day. The secretary wanted us to sit with him and Dr. Saaid in the viewing stands, which were set up for a big celebration and parade to take place the next day. My wife and I talked it over for some time, but decided to turn down the great honor — about like deciding not to sit with our own president at a state function. Our apology was

The tower (steeple) of St. James church in Medjugorje, Yugoslavia (now Croatia), with a group of pilgrims from our church. It was our intent to thank God for surviving an auto crash. I also wanted to measure ELF waves, and the paramagnetic properties of the Croatian mountain called Mount Podbrodo where, on June 24, 1981, the Virgin appeared to six young visionaries. The Medjugorje apparition is still occuring to a few of the visionaries. It has become as famous as Lourdes among the Catholic believers of miracles. At exactly 5:45 the visionaries were praying in the steeple of St. James when I arrived with Jerry Hale and his video camera. After measuring the steeple I, a laser expert, stepped back and recorded with my camera the experiment. As usual, because of the dim light, I took two photos (1/30 & 1/60 sec.). The first photo showed only a lighted church steeple, in the second, 5 "laser" lines came from a tower window and converged on a couple praying below. At the same exact time (recorded on the video camera), Jerry Hale's tape showed the lowest window to be in total darkness! As an authority on biological laser radiation, I must leave it to my readers to figure out this message to me and mankind. "Light is the light of darkness!" — St. John.

with our own president at a state function. Our apology was given and our reason was accepted.

We had promised Winnie's sister, Teresa, who is a nun in Newcastle, England, that on our way to Ireland we would stop and visit her in her convent. If we had stayed in Egypt, we would have to change our tickets and fly directly to Ireland, a big disappointment for her. We left Egypt that same night, the only passengers except for one other man, on the late-night 727 flight for London. We landed, slept late in a hotel, and took the mid-morning train to Newcastle.

While talking to Sister Teresa, she asked if we had met Sadat. We told her how we had turned down meeting him so we could have a short visit with her in Newcastle. She turned pale, or least I think she did. She showed us the morning paper. Sadat and twenty or thirty people had been assassinated. The secretary of agriculture was killed, and Dr. Saaid critically wounded. He was flown to Walter Reed Hospital in the United States to try to save his life.

We met him once again a few years later when he invited us and our friend, the pyramid expert Patrick Flanagan, to his house for tea. Dr. Saaid told us that if we had stayed in Egypt that extra day, both Winnie and myself would be dead since the area was well sprinkled with machine gun fire.

Again the skeptic may say, "just coincidental." Coincidence is the cop-out word of our materialistic society.

Those with common sense and a belief in higher power will agree with Winnie and me that, through Mary's intercession, Divine Providence had once again held out His hand for us. He had done it through Winnie's sister, a nun.

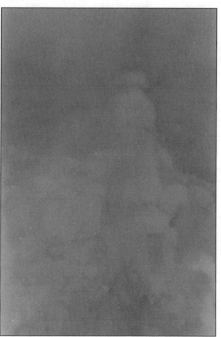

During the fall of 1995, Winnie and I visited Fatima. I carried my paintbox explorer's kit instead of my camera. On the last day of our visit, I bought a Fuji "throwaway" camera and took two photos, I do not know why, of the first apparation site of the three little shepherd visionaries. This is the rocky place where an angel appeared to the three children. The first photo showed a statue, the second is totally inexpicable. It shows an exact "ghostly," cloud-like figure of the statue and children. Since the disposable camera has a fixed focus and shutter speed, there is no way to explain this photo. I took the camera apart and the shutter worked fine. It could not be slowed down to cause an overexposure, which, in any case, would not look the same. The hand of God.

CHAPTER XI
Holographic Rocks

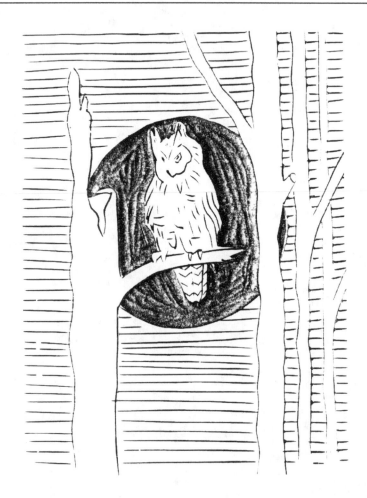

Rock art, then, is an important means of reaching some understanding of the sacred dimensions and certain related practices of the prehistoric period.

Indian Rock Art of the Southwest
Polly Schaasafsma

I have often wondered if the smell of good coffee at sunrise is addictive. I doubt it because as Dr. M. Scott Peck, M.D. states in his marvelous book, *In Search of Stones* (1):

> *Yesterday I suggested that in seeking romance outside of marriage I was foolishly seeking a substitute for God. So it is with virtually all addictions. They are forms of idolatry. For the alcoholic, the bottle becomes an idol; for the heroin addict, the drug is his god. The non drug addictions are no different. Our whole society may be going down the tubes because of its idolatry of wealth and security.*

True addiction leads to misery and destruction. Coffee at sunrise leads only to a calming expectation of a brand new day of God's life.

My son-in-law, Byron, was just pouring the coffee as I walked into the kitchen. He offered me a cup. As was usual, I was the only early riser at the six a.m. sunrise time that began his journey to work. Byron is a tall, gentle mechanical genius whose job is to keep the wheels of America turning. It is men such as he that keep the sunrise brighter on days such as the one we had planned.

If I have any addiction at all, it is the same one outlined so beautifully by M. Scott Peck in his masterful description of the mystic properties of stone. I love rocks.

On this day of the winter solstice, Dec. 22, 1995, I puttered around the house waiting for the rest of the family, my wife Winnie, Colette, my youngest daughter, and my son Kevin, to arise and wake up the five grandchildren.

The sun was beginning to reflect off the snow that had covered the crest of the Sandia Mountains the night before. My most obliging daughter, as delightful a person as her husband Byron, had promised to drive the family to a magic place called by the locals Boca Negra Canyon — Black Rock Canyon (Boca really means mouth).

Colette's high-ceilinged and airy home sits among the cedars and pinion trees of Cedar Crest facing the backside of the great pink-granite Sandia range. The steep red cliffs on the opposite side of that range envelope the eastern edge of Albuquerque. We would have to drive around the south end of the Sandias, and clear across the city to reach Boca Negra, which was on the opposite side of the Rio Grande River.

Just as the white snow of the distant peaks turned red-orange from diffused sunlight, and just as those magic beams of energy enveloped the room, five grandchildren — three for Colette and two for Kevin — appeared as if by magic. Some were still sleepy-eyed and some, as the well known Western saying goes, were "raring to go."

Like the sunrise light, they also enveloped my being with their own special child-like energy. It was a fitting day to start on a small exploration of the black rocks of Boca Negra Canyon.

Soon my Winnie and Colette were through making breakfast for everyone, and we were on our way.

Boca Negra was almost a lost national monument. The city of Albuquerque spreads across the Rio Grande and up the slopes of the west side to the volcanic rim of the black rocks that face the river. A huge subdivision actually edges the national monument, and might have, if allowed, blasted itself right up the slope of rocks where the national monument now stands. It was only the outcry of sensible Indian advocates and archaeologists that stopped the addiction-like power and greed of thoughtless land speculators and other such idolators of wealth (2).

Boca Negra was saved for one very good reason; it is the largest "rock-book" of Indian petroglyphs in the Northern

Hemisphere. There were over 15,000 Indian petroglyphs chipped into the black basalt rocks that line many miles along the black ridge overlooking the Rio Grande River.

I have a firm belief in what the Christian religion calls Divine Providence, which I understand to mean that although we have a free will, God actually directs our life by placing in our path certain choices. In the majority of cases people of good will, which includes most of the human population, take the correct path outlined by God. Evil occurs when a certain few chose the wrong path — "devilish providence" one might say.

Divine Providence was working this Christmas season, the day of the winter solstice, 1995. The federal government (or at least part of it) had been shut down due to the greed and power of a few, led by some feelingless "trickle down" politicians. Using the so-called deficit, which does not exist because we owe it to ourselves, they laid plans to starve the poor and motherless and to sabotage the environmental gains of the previous years (2).

The state of New Mexico had outwitted the government. They put aside extra money to keep its wonderful attractions open by hiring a few non-federal attendants at such parks as Carlsbad Caverns and Boca Negra.

They reasoned correctly that the attractions would bring in more money than they lost by hiring temporary people — Divine Providence at work as far as we were concerned. When we drove up to the national monument, the gate was open. The cheerful state gatekeeper gave us a well-illustrated pamphlet on the history of Boca Negra Canyon. On the cover of the pamphlet was a drawing of the macaw for which the second park trail was named, "Macaw Trail." By far the most interesting petroglyphs, however, lay along the Mesa Point Trail.

This trail climbs the steep boulder-strewn side of a mesa-like peninsula that takes the shape of a keyhole sticking out from the surrounding steep, rock-strewn ridge. At the top is a flat, open peak with a ring of black boulders. This rock-walled area is considered by some archaeologists to be an ancient ceremonial area. They are no doubt correct, for such magic high places were often sacred to the Indians. A continuous breeze blows across the surface of the flat-topped mesa. The "spirit of God's breath," the Indians would call it. I have also heard mans' breath called the "spirit of life."

As we scrambled slowly up the steep trail observing the rock-chipped figures, we began to attempt to interpret them. The most obvious figures were those of the local wildlife. One easily recognized figure, like that of the macaw, is a civet cat. This animal is neither a civet nor cat, but a member of the raccoon family. It is also known as a raccoon fox or mountain cat. It dwells mainly in the dry deserts of the Southwest from Mexico to Colorado. It is recognized by its big ears, pointed muzzle, broad furry legs, and large broad tail. Its main habitat is the same type of stone-strewn slope that we were climbing.

Although common to such rocky areas, it is doubtful that the Indians hunted and ate the animal. Taken young, they make wonderful pets as they are gentle and easily tamed. The Pueblo Indians are great pet keepers as the macaw indicated. The macaw figure is interesting because it not only shows the large bird, but also below it a caged parrot. It is known from the historical literature that the Pueblo Indians traded far into tropical Mexico for parrots. There is little doubt that macaws, besides being interesting pets, were kept primarily for their molted feathers, useful in ceremonial dress.

The next figure that I studied in detail illustrated what might best be described as a children's "kachina" ceremony. A kachina, in simplified terms, is an Indian "saint." The "spirit

The civit cat is a denizen of the rocky hills of the Southwest. It is a desert member of the raccoon family with big ears and a long, ringed tail. The Indians, no doubt, kept is as a pet. Top photo is a rock petroglyph of the animal.

saint" represents something in nature, like corn or an owl. During ceremonies Indian adults dress like the kachina "saints" and make kachina dolls for little girls. The boys get bows and arrows. Girls save their kachina dolls. White people collect them. In the left section of the figure is depicted a drummer, in the center a pigtailed child, and to the right what well might be the tribe's three-horned kachina, similar to the kachina of the Hopi Indians. The figure has round eyes, an oval mouth, and three rods stick up from a square face. The three-horned kachina is thought by experts to be a Zuni kachina introduced into the first mesa of the Hopi villages. If so, it well may be a kachina that was common to many pueblos in distant times. The Zuni dwell not far from Black Rock. Be that as it may, it is obviously a ceremonial drawing set off by the natural squares of the cracked rocks.

Petroglyph experts believe that each square represents an area. We thus have a drum area, children's area and kachina area. Anyone is welcome to their own interpretation, but if they consider the images other than ceremonial drawings they probably do not know much about Pueblo Indians, nature or kachinas. The long-legged frog below the drummer, without a doubt, represents the Rio Grande River, a few miles away.

As the park guide pamphlet points out, most of the petroglyphs scattered along the seventeen miles of rim rocks represent the Rio Grande style. This style developed between the 13th and 16th centuries during the construction of many Indian pueblos along the river. Common images include flute players, drummers and dancers, wildlife, clouds, hills and stars. A ceremony on a magic, or sacred, mesa top a few miles from the river would bring along the water by representing it with a frog coming from where frogs occur. The three-horned kachina is thought to be the bean growth (water) kachina.

The pueblo itself probably existed between 1300 and 1600 somewhere along the river. The Pueblo Indians were farmers, not nomadic hunters. They planted mainly beans, squash and corn, grown along the fertile valley. They also hunted the uplands above the escarpment for rabbits, antelope and local game birds.

Since I am an ornithologist and falconer, for me the most interesting discovery of our day was a beautifully executed map and quail hunting scene. The map tells one immediately where to find the quail.

A zig-zag line is known by petroglyph experts to represent clouds. Above the Indian area (map), delineated by the square (map margins), is a zig-zag cloud symbol, and also a line representing the horizon. Just below is a broad-winged buteo or golden eagle. Both are hunting birds (see *Peterson's Bird Guide, Silhouette of Birds of Prey*). Next to this soaring predator is the worldwide symbol for sun and sky (the universe, a circle with a dot in the middle). This figure also shows the four compass directions. As is true of most things, both mystical and Indian, the map top is orientated east towards the sun and not north as we non-Indians would have it.

Within this area are a mountain (bottom), a smaller half mountain (right), and a peninsula mesa (top) sticking out from the left. At the tip of the mesa is a rectangular figure (square) representing an area.

Between the peninsula mesa and the half mountain are a four-legged animal and two-winged bird. The square area at the end of the north peninsula mesa, no doubt, represents the ceremonial area on top of black rock mesa. A photo of my wife, son, and grandchildren that was taken there shows two volcanic peaks (one half mountain left, and whole mountain right) rising in the distance.

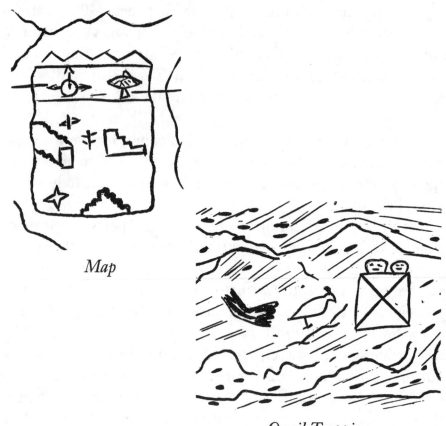

Map

Quail Trapping

Kachina Ceremony

Since the animal and bird life lie between the half mountain and the ceremonial mesa, the hunting areas lie at that place. It is an area where, on that very day, I saw a common red-tailed buteo soaring over the water tank in the distance.

Between the whole mountain and the ceremonial mesa, a bright star arises at night. All petroglyph experts agree that the four-pointed cross in the lower left represents a star. The bright evening or morning stars probably arise over this horizon during the hunting seasons.

The high plateau area delineated by the "hunter's map" is a dry plateau. According to the anthropologists, the Pueblo Indians, who were mainly farmers, constructed agricultural terraces along parts of the rock escarpment in order to build up soil, and slow water runoff from summer storms. They hunted game birds and animals with the bow. According to the Boca Negra pamphlet, it is known that they also set traps. There are two Indian drawings that show an obviously good quail-trapping area.

Any bird watcher will agree that birds are located best by call. The first figure indicates a hunter (kachina head) with big ears for hearing. To his left are sounds issuing from a flute, indicating noise. Below the sound is a walking bird (two legs) with a huge top-knot feather. Above the flute is a flying bird. There is absolutely no question as to the identity of the walking bird. The only Southwestern bird with such a top-knot is the Gimbel's quail. The natural habitat of the Gimbel's quail is the dry upland semideserts of the southwest from Mexico to southern Colorado. It is especially common along the dry edge of the Rio Grande.

From my younger days in the southwest deserts, I am well acquainted with the strange cha-chea-cha-chea call of this almost invisible bird. Quail hunters dislike the bird as it refuses to fly, although it is fully capable of doing so. It occurs in

At top, a petroglyph of an Indian hunting scout (big ears) listening for Gimbel's quail. To the left of his head is an indian flute with sound "lines" between a walking quail and a flying quail. At bottom, the head of two Indians peek over the edge of a blind at a Gimbel's quail being driven toward the blind by a beater (foot).

148   *My Search for Traces of God*

large coveys of twenty to thirty birds that run along the ground through the thick semidesert brush. This makes them exceedingly difficult to see. If not for their strange call, they might go unnoticed. It also makes for difficult bow and arrow hunting.

There is no question that it is a quail-trapping scene. The method would be similar to the one I used for trapping kestrels to train in falconry — bait a pullover net with a mouse and wait in a blind to pull the net over the falcon as it strikes.

The second hunting petroglyph shows two Indians hiding behind such a blind. As with grouse shooters on a Scottish moorland, beaters, symbolized by a foot, are driving the Gimbel's quail toward some corn or grain scattered on the ground in front of the blind.

The scene brought back with considerable nostalgia my days trapping kestrels and hunting for hawks' nests. Trapping techniques are the same world wide — today and yesterday.

One of the kachina rock pictures resembles Mongawa Wu-ute, the old woman kachina. He wears a woman's costume and dances with her children — two or three screech owls. The screech owl has two feathered tufts called horns. This is one of the two-horned kachinas.

Strangly enough Mongawa Wu-ute dances mainly in the bean dance. Since the bean was the main source of protein among desert tribes (where meat is so scarce), this must have been one of the most important kachina ceremonies.

My love of the little screech owl goes back to our house on Menands Road by the Sage estate where one gave its plaintive call from the woods by the estate gatehouse. The screech owl does not screech but warbles its low hoot. The little screech owl is one of the most mystic of birds, both to me and to the Indians.

The winter solstice, which is also my wife's birthday, is sacred to many ancients. We planned a special dinner to celebrate Winnie's birthday. Astrologists would no doubt consider December 22 a great day to enter the world.

As we started down the steep slope, three rather strange figures caught my attention. On the climb up I had ignored these circles and straight lines.

I lagged behind my five scampering grandchildren, and stopped to photograph the petroglyphs. One figure was a decreasing spiral that looked like rings from a rock splashing in water. The other figures were stones or circles with parallel lines extending out from them. Some lines emerged from one direction, some from all four directions. They reminded me of bursts of rays seen reflected from camera lenses, or electric lights seen through squinted eyelids.

These are most certainly the ancient pictographs that are more difficult to interpret than the pragmatic ceremonial and hunting scenes. The images transport one from the domestic domain of day-to-day life across mystic barriers to the realm of the spirit — and God.

My mind drifted back to the same strange symbols seen at ancient rock sites all over the world. I call them eye-squinting sun symbols as they are easily duplicated by squinting at any bright source of light.

As we drove home, I mentally planned some experiments with a candle, a flashlight and a laser. These mystical symbols appeared to float on those black rocks like some holographic laser form from the mystical past.

CHAPTER XII
Laser Light from God

I believe in one God, the Father Almighty
Maker of heaven and earth
And of all things visible and invisible.

Book of Common Prayer
Church of England

A candle, like the hot electric heating element of your kitchen stove, gives off visible light. The candle flickers, but the stove element does not. It is the flicker that makes the candle so much more attractive than the stove top.

The flicker seems to hold one's eyes and, as every romantic couple knows, attract one to the never-neverland of romance. It is a symbol of love, and many religions burn candles as a means of setting the mind on a path of love toward God or God's human mother, Mary.

My theory is that the candle lures a person to thoughts of God's light of love because, in the invisible region, it gives off hundreds upon hundreds of narrow molecules vibrating at frequencies of far-infrared radiation. They are a part of God's invisible world. These infrared lines are so strong and so narrow that they are almost like hundreds of little lasers. That is why I call them "maser-like" — for molecular amplification of stimulated emission light (IR). I was the first researcher to ever plot this phenomenon in the spectrum.

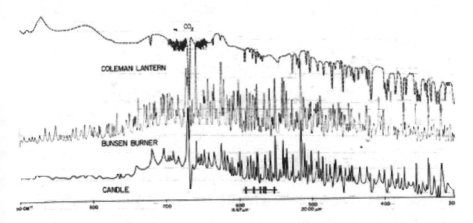

Infrared spectrum of candle (bottom), Bunsen burner (middle), and Coleman lantern (top). The lantern shows no narrow-band emission as it burns too hot. Candle and Bunsen burner both show the narrow, infrared bands that are generated in the flame from water vapor. Note the broader curve that they ride on, it represents the broad-band heat curve of the infrared. Some of the narrow lines are the same as frequencies coming from the scent that attracts insects.

The Buddhists know well that these candle far-infrared frequencies have both calming and healing power. That is why they use them to heal sick elephants and people.

From the earliest of times, candles were utilized by the Christian religion. The ceremonial candlelight for evening prayer was called the *Lucernarium* in Latin. It is the forerunner of our modern Paschal candle.

There is evidence that candles were used at mass as early as the 7th century. In the 11th century candles appeared on the altar table. In the Catholic religion, candles should be 65% beeswax. Although my research has shown that modern paraffin candles give off the same far-infrared narrow-band emission as beeswax candles, the beeswax frequencies are always stronger. A wise church in some matters . . .

We may now understand that the hundreds of types of wax molecules are vibrating from the heat to produce these candle frequencies. Since both plants and insects are coated with a thin layer of wax, many of these lines are the exact same frequencies that the insect is attracted to from plant scents and sex scents.

It is most certainly a sad fact that many local bishops have "gone modern" and moved Mary and her votive candles away from her son at the altar. The bishops were not told by the Vatican Council to do so, but because of a materialistic bent they have decided that such outward signs of worship are superstitious — best to hide it in a corner.

I am told by more than one modern theologian that having Mary's statue and votive candles at the altar detracts from the cross above the tabernacle. I am still waiting for some great scholar to explain how having a "photograph" of a mother beside her son detracts from "sonhood."

I have yet to meet a faithful Catholic, or Protestant for that matter, who believes moving Mary from beside her Son contributes to a more holy worship.

It is well known that English-speaking bishops are unreasonably afraid of miracles, for in the entire life of the English-speaking church not a single apparition has ever been approved. Why? (1) I believe it is because of a subsconcious fear of earthly signs from God — in short, pride.

The visible radiation and warm infrared that comes from the burning candle is very broadband, like a mountain seen in the distance. It is the visible and heat radiation (infrared) output that is seen as a broad curve by a low-resolution spectrophotometer, an instrument for detecting radiation. The energy from this broad curve of "heat" is incoherent, and goes out in all directions. The narrow-band emissions are contained in the broadband heat, and can only be seen with a high-resolution Fourier transform spectrophotometer. They are like seeing the tall pine trees against the distant mountainside. The pines are the narrow lines.

mountains

trees

I first detected these narrow-band frequencies with the high-resolution instrument. I now know for certain that by producing some of these frequencies electronically, in the IR and radio (and sound) region, one can heal almost any disease. Yes, candles give off both ELF (extremely low frequency) radio and sound along with IR and visible radiation. Besides candle IR, there is a second concept of infrared and light photon physics that we must understand. It is called *interference* by physicists. It involves the photon rings of energy that go out in concentric circles when a photon hits some objects. Astronomers call them Airy's rings, named after their 18th century discoverer. Chemists call the pheonomena *interference patterns* and physicists call them *target waves*. It is most unfortunate that each speciality makes up its own terminology in order to confuse the nonspecialist. Airy's rings, target waves, and interference patterns are all exactly the same thing. Such circular patterns are depicted in all rock art.

Interference in physics is easiest to understand by visualizing throwing two rocks in the water next to each other. In the center, where the rock hits, is a clear space. From the space large, and then smaller and smaller, waves go out in a circle like a target. These differ from archery targets in that they get closer and closer together, and less and less high (amplitude) as the energy dissipates.

We may easily understand that as the wave circles approach each other they "interfere" with each other.

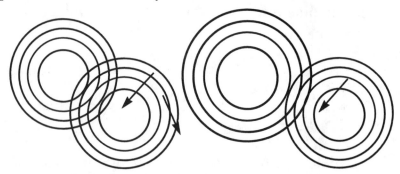

In terms of religion and theology we might call the bright spaces God's life area and the black regions the unknown mystical area.

> *In Him was life; and life was the light of man*
> *And the light shineth in darkness and the darkness*
> *comprehended it not.*
>
> John 1:4-5

We Catholics used to end our beautiful Latin mass with those words. Unfortunately, in the '60s, not only were these remarkable words dropped, so was the universal Latin. With that worldwide liturgy we Catholics could feel right at home no matter where God's direction landed us. I say direction (like pointing the way) because God does not will us to do anything. God only directs our path by Divine Revelation, or by signs called miracles.

Airy's rings were reproduced by physicists by shooting a beam of electrons at a TV-like screen. When the electrons hit the screen, as they were emitted from a heated element, they cause "splash" rings on the screen. The rings are seen as dark and light spaces. The technical term is an interference pattern. When the waves are together (addition) there is light; when they are not together (subtract) there is dark — thus the target effect. Airy's circles prove not only the wave theory of light, but also the particle quantum theory, because the bands of dark and light can be seen to be composed of small particles (spots).

I repeated the exact same experiment with photons (light) instead of electrons (electricity). I shot photons at Kodacolor or Fujicolor film to produce photographic Airy's rings.

It has been theorized that when one photon hits a detector of any type it changes to two photons. This is a strange phenomenon that is very difficult to understand, but which I proved as an experimental fact. With my equipment I also demonstrated, as Einstein said, that time is curved over billions of miles (special relativity). It is also curved right on my desktop over inches, as Einstein did *not* say (see Epilogue and appendix). I designed my photon film experiment to show how a very strange photograph I obtained could be constructed by God utilizing the natural physics He designed.

The image is a strange, holographic-looking photo of the face of the Virgin Mary with her hands folded. I obtained it

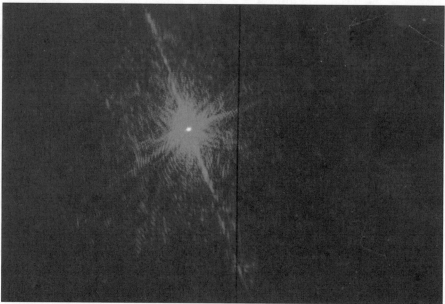

At top, Earth Sun symbol. It is the "squinting" sun symbol with one ray going toward the earth and the rest to the four compass directions. At bottom, my laser radiation copy of this same figure. Note the Airy's rings going out from it, and the fact that, although the laser was pointed directly at the split image circle in the center of the camera, it has moved 1.6 cm from the center of the film. *Detector Surface Timespace Movement.* (See appendix).

without knowing how one day in my lab. The mystic face precisely resembles the Virgin of Guadalupe.

The face appeared floating behind and slightly to the left of a candle flame I was working with (see block cut at chapter heading). I was measuring radiation emission from the flame with a Geiger radiation counter. The detector of the counter was to the side of of the flame on a Navajo rug covering my desktop (2).

When the film came back from the processing lab, I showed it to Winnie. The head had appeared as if by magic on my roll of Fujicolor film.

On a trip to the Amazon in Peru the previous month, I had discovered that the tobacco a Shaman was using to cure a little Achuara headhunter girl of a high fever and earache was slightly radioactive. The large roll of tobacco he gave me measured 60 to 70 counts per minute. Normal background gamma radiation in Florida is 14 to 20 counts per minute and the same is true on the Huagramona River where the tribe lived. The smoke he used for healing was a mixture of tobacco smoke and the scent from a tree called "jungle garlic." He blew it while shaking a palm leaf at the face of the sick little girl nursing at her mother's breast. Within minutes the watering-eyed, ear-tugging child sat up and started laughing. I felt her forehead — the fever had disappeared — the magic of Shamanism.

I had been recording the radiation count from the Shaman's tobacco and from a candle in my lab when I took the photo for a record of the experiment. There was no image of the Virgin's head behind the candle then.

"What a beautiful photograph," Winnie exclaimed when I showed it to her. "How did you get that?"

How did I get it? I had not the slightest idea, but we both agreed it was unique, and, in all likelihood a message from God.

The Virgin in the candle. Prior to my last trip to the Amazon to visit the Achuara "headhunters," I obtained a photo of the Virgin's bust floating in the candle flame I was measuring with my Geiger counter. To receive such a candle photo "mystery" hologram there must be two sources of coherent laser radiation. I believe one set of partially coherent photons came directly from the candle, and the second set from coherent natural Cabannes scatter radiation from some resonating surface in my laboratory, *e.g.*, the flash or window screens with angled sunlight on them. Thus could God will a Mary "hologram" in order to ease my wife's fear that I might disappear forever in the deep jungles of the Amazon. The Virgin's face is clearer in the original color print. It loses by converting to black and white photograph.

What made the incident of the Virgin in the candle even more strange was that I was working on an experiment and praying at the same time. The Geiger counter was pointed at the candle flame because, after years of studying moth activity around candles, I had never measured a wax-generated flame to see if its count was higher than the tobacco radiation — it was not.

Since I always document my experiments on film, I snapped a flash photo of the experimental set up. A carved, wooden bust of the Virgin was nowhere near the candle, although it did sit on my desk.

When I returned from Harmon's photo lab, I was surprized to see the candle-flame-generated face of Mary.

I had planned on continuing my work along the Hugramona River (River of the Tapers) with my Achuara headhunter Shaman friend. Winnie did not want me to return for a third trip. She was not concerned about the so-called "headhunting" Achuara tribe as I had convinced her they were a very gentle, lovable people. Their village was a grass-roofed paradise. Her concern was the single-engine bush flight over five-hundred miles of virgin, trackless jungles.

That corner of Peru, jutting northward toward Ecuador, covers 25,000 square miles of swampy rain forest. If one loses an engine there is no way out, even if one survived the crash. We were the first to visit the Achuara tribe (3).

On the previous trip, a strange weather phenomenon had forced us to make an emergency landing on a small curving river. The clouds lowered to 700 feet just above the forest canopy, and hundreds of pillars of smoky-looking clouds soon covered the overcast ceiling to the forest tree tops. It was a weather phenomenon of the rainforest that only a very few bush pilots have ever witnessed. Jets are above any overcast, and the thick forest canopy shields the phenomenon from ground vision.

As we were forced lower and lower, we were soon twisting and turning between the white pillars of energy — almost as if flying between the stone pillars of the Parthenon in Athens. We made a safe water landing, and waited two or three hours until the string clouds lifted. I named them "fairy string clouds" as I could envision thousands of jungle fairies dropping their fishing lines from above into the jungle.

Because the narrow river twisted and turned along the jungle course, we would not get enough of a run to gain air speed. I was flying copilot. I watched in dismay as the tachometer crossed the green at 3,500 rpm and pegged the needle at 4,000 rpm in the red.

In a peculiarity of South America politics, our pilot was an Air Force major and the aircraft belonged to the Air Force. I, an American civilian, had rented a Peruvian Air Force aircraft. To this day, I believe the Peruvian Government wanted to see what would happen to us if we actually contacted the Achuara tribe.

My two friends, Paul Beaver, an ornithologist who works in Peru, and Kenneth Silver, with whom I traveled across Europe in the late '40s, were with me. Kenneth, like me, had just retired from the federal government.

After a run of several miles following the twisting river, the major pulled back the stick. I fully expected the engine to blow. As the nose climbed, I watched the jungle at the end of the last curve coming straight at us. The pontoons hung a foot or so above the 150-foot canopy as we climbed over the forest (4).

When we returned home, Kenneth wrote about our head-hunter adventure in great and scary detail, as only an ex-journalist could. Needless to say, after she read the story, further jungle trips worried Winnie to no end.

For Winnie's peace of mind, I had decided not to return to the rainforest when Mary appeared in my candle flame as if in answer to my prayers. Winnie and I looked upon the unlikely photo as a sign from God. It told us that I would be under Mary's protection.

Long years of studying coherent, in-phase radiation, which I termed maser-like, had led me to believe that low-energy coherent photons in nature are not only a mechanism in life and healing, but also (as in my photo) utilized in God's earthly messages. Religious people would call such messages from God *signs*. By whatever name, I do believe in messages from God. I do not believe, as many theologians do, that God talking back to the prayerful is at all rare. In fact, I believe that God speaks to everyone at one time or another, it is just that most do not pray enough to get the message — until it is too late.

It is one of the most disturbing idiosyncrasies of mankind that, as the gentle philosopher C.S. Lewis has aptly pointed out, if one talks to God it is prayer, but if God speaks back to one, the person to whom God speaks is considered strange. Of course, as long as one speaks the truth with love of God and neighbor, it little matters if one is considered different. Both the great scientist, Oppenheimer, and the great priest, St. Francis, were most certainly considered strange. Perhaps I am a little strange also, since I believe that science should lead one to God and not to greedy materialism.

EPILOGUE
It All Comes Together

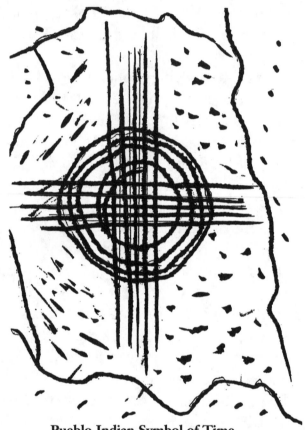

Pueblo Indian Symbol of Time

Almost certainly God is not in time. His life does not consist of moments following one another. If a million people are praying to Him at ten-thirty tonight, He need not listen to them all in that one little snippet which we call ten-thirty. Ten-thirty and every other moment from the beginning of the world — is always the present for Him.

Mere Christianity
C. S. Lewis

God is timeless, or at least so the theologians maintain. It would appear that the great English popular philosopher of Christianity, C.S. Lewis, agrees.

In my research, which is the biophysics of life, time is very much a factor. Scientists tend to worry considerably about time. It is Einstein's concept of time that made the scourge of life, the atomic bomb, work.

In a nutshell, two half globes of critical mass, uranium or plutonium, had to be driven together as a perfect fit, in a very small fraction of a second.

$$E = mc^2$$

E, of course, is energy, m is mass, and c is the speed of light squared. In math terms:

$$4 = 2 \times 2$$

A very simple, but also a very elegant concept.

Everyone knows that speed depends on time and space, *e.g.* miles (space) per hour (time), or meters per second.

Space is measured by micrometers, millimeters, centimeters, kilometers (miles), etc. In short, distance measures space.

The definition of time is well fixed in science, so it should not be difficult to understand that if one makes a fixed figure, like a candle, move from left to right or up or down by changing only time, then one is "measuring" space with time alone, and can thus determine if space and time are really curved as Einstein maintained. He called it *spacetime*, not *space time*. One adjusts to the other.

Einstein maintained that time was curved only over millions upon millions of miles due to the gravitational pull of the mighty sun. Unlike me, he did not consider it curved at short distances, for instance, over my desktop.

Like the Virgin Mary, I love birds. As a young man taking photographs of birds' nests at close range with the early slow, black-and-white film, I noticed that in dark swamps, where I

Least bittern nesting in a swamp along the Mohawk River in New York, near Albany where I lived after the war. I took this photo in the spring of 1946 and noted that the edge of the swamp moved when I bracketed the exposures by changing time speeds. I was convinced, at that time, that I had moved the tripod on the camera.

photographed birds like the least bittern, the edge of the film always seemed different if I bracketed the film with a series of exposures. I bracketed such photos, usually in dark swamps, because light intensity was low. In the early days, both black-and-white and Kodacolor film were much slower.

I was young and inexperienced, so I let those in the "know" convince me that I, in all likelihood, had moved the tripod while focusing on the ground glass. More than one scientist has missed out on a really significient experiment by allowing colleagues to convince him or her that their interpretation of a natural event was an artifact and not a real natural event.

I designed an experiment to retest moving space. What I obtained convinced me that my image in the candle flame was a natural hologram instigated by God. If I could move space (a photographic image) with time, and also prove a two-photon system, I would have a natural mechanism for moving the wooden bust of the Virgin from somewhere on my desk to the candle flame. The shutter speed would do it.

A hologram requires two coherent beams. One beam would be the light from the candle, illuminating the bust somewhere on my desk, and the other beam was natural Cabannes scatter reflected accidentally (at God's command) off of some surface in the room either from my flash, or perhaps sunlight scattered from the window frame beyond my desk. The two beams, each of two synchronized photons, would focus the natural hologram on the film behind the candle flame — God ordered it.

In the appendix, I have provided the first paper of an experiment showing space (an image) can be moved in a curve by time alone. The curve, when plotted, turns out to be a sine wave. In short, time goes along in waves just like Airy's rings. When time is plotted against space in my experiment, it is shown to be a sine wave. A sine wave consists of a half circle above a zero line, another half circle connected at zero, and below the line.

If we plot the image of the laser beam or candle, we see that they move along with the shutter speed alone (time). I believe the *positive* top of the wave is our world, and the bottom is the *negative* portion of the world where mystical things happen (the scientifically inclined should read my paper in the appendix).

I also believe that coherent scatter, called Cabannes scatter, is extremely common in nature and causes, at God's will, the laser lines I have seen from sacred places with my color films.

My photographs, included in this book as black-and-white photos, will be deposited in the American Heritage Library at the University of Wyoming. Even after I am dead these photographs can easily be examined at that library.

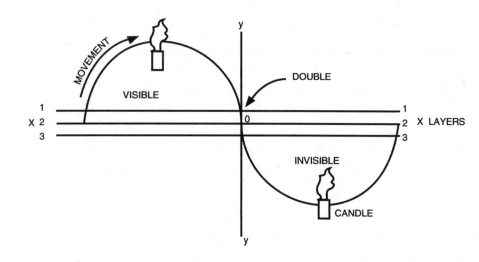

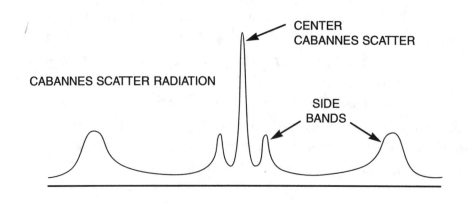

Visible and infrared Cabannes scatter (coherent) radiation goes out from many different surfaces, just like the radio waves from a transmitter. They even have sidebands of radiation.

God could easily will such radiation to scatter in such a manner as to expose sensitive three-layer film, and also in such a manner, because of the sine wave character of time, to produce a natural hologram such as my candle Virgin image.

I have often thought back on my early bird photos and wondered if I really moved the ground glass camera or if time really moves space. My experiment proved the latter (see appendix).

The fact that space can be moved by changing only time is irrefutable.

The mystic symbol of the Pueblo Indians, shown in this chapter block cut, is obviously a symbol of time and space recorded by astute Native Americans. The circles are Airy's waves so easily seen by squinting one's eyes, and the lines are beams of light shooting from those waves. The symbol states, in no uncertain terms, that time travels both in waves and also in straight parallel lines ($\sim\sim\sim\sim$ $\longrightarrow$).

It was quite easy for me to obtain this symbolic figure by shooting a helium-neon laser beam through my pinhole Nikon camera onto three-layered Fuji or Kodacolor film. As is evident to those of a scientific mind who have read my paper in the appendix, space plotted against time is a sine wave — thus the significance of the Pueblo Indian's symbol.

What this says is that for the speed of light to remain constant ($\longrightarrow$), spacetime must constantly adjust itself (like waves $\sim\sim\sim\sim$). Big waves lengthen time, little waves shorten time, so that on Earth the speed of light (which depends on time) remains constant. I was the first to prove this with my simple experiment — laser, candle and pinhole camera.

What does my sine wave paper have to do with the mystical worlds of religion and God?

This is not a book on science, but rather book on Divine Providence. The events of my life led to the paper given in the appendix, and to my monograph on the image of the Virgin of Guadalupe as well as my work on the Shroud of Turin.

Those papers say that the science of physics can be utilized experimentally to produce the mystic photograph I have obtained as well as the cloth images of the Shroud and Tilma. The parallel lines of the Indian time symbol are the same type of parallel lines that I obtained coming from the visionaries steeple in Medjugorje. They are generated by coherent or partially coherent radiation scattered off of various natural surfaces. God ordered it.

It will take an entire technical book to explain in detail both the laser lines from God, and the holographic image of the Virgin in the candle flame.

Miraculous pictures have been taken at special places by prayerful, faithful people all over the world. Hundreds of such mystic photographs have been obtained on Holy Hill in Conyers, Georgia, where the true visionary Nancy Fowler has seen the Blessed Mother for the past several years on the thirteenth of each month. I do not have a chapter on apparitions at Conyers for the simple reason that my friend, Dr. Ramon Sanchez, is writing a book on that subject. There are several superb scientists studying Nancy Fowler. Conyers is an American Fatima. The Shroud of Turin and Virgin of Guadalupe are also examples of God's willing images as messages to man.

With regard to the candle image of the Virgin Mary being a hologram, the paper in the appendix demonstrates the possibility in no uncertain terms.

I do not intend to write a technical chapter on holograms, but the simple, irrefutable fact is that in order for a hologram to form, two coherent beams (or a split beam) are needed (see double candle flame in the spacetime paper in appendix).

My paper, given in the appendix, proves conclusively that every time a photon hits a three-layered detector, like film, plant leaf, human skin, etc., it becomes two synchronized, coherent photons. This says that life processes are coherent-holographic, especially the brain, as Drs. Penfield and Pritman postulated years ago.

The skeptic will say that my work proves all miracles are understandable. That is decidedly not true, one miracle that is not understandable by man is Christ raising Himself (and others) from the dead. God then utilized the ultimate miracle of life itself.

My paper proves beyond a doubt that space (an image) moves as a sine wave. In my book on paramagnetism, readers can observe an Airy's (diffraction) wave from the side instead of from above. These waves are in the 1 to 300 Hz range (changing like ripples), and are generated in the atmosphere. They are extremely strong at mystical spots where the Virgin has appeared. I detect them with a piece of burlap soaked in sea water for an antenna — both natural substances. I may end by pointing out that these type of healing waves are especially strong in churches where people are praying.

I may also state with certainty that all of the events of my life led directly to my studies of the Shroud of Turin, and studies on the Virgin of Guadalupe. The later work was published by a Catholic Research Organization called CARA (see bibliography).

Because I believe, as did St. Augustine, that miracles are not only signs from God, but are also temporal, or of this world, I can do little better than quote C.S. Lewis one more time:

> *Every event which might claim to be a miracle is in the last resort, something presented to our senses, heard, touched, smelled, or tasted. And our senses are not infallible. If anything extraordinary seems to have happened, we can always say that we have been the victims of an illusion. If we hold a philosophy which excludes the supernatural, this is what we always shall say. What we learn depends on the kind of philosophy we bring to experience.*

The materialistic scientists, corrupted by pride, ego, and in some cases greed (grants), will say my life is a long series of coincidences and that I suffer from delusions. Those who believe in angels will read this book with joy.

My studies of Mary led to the discovery of the paramagnetic force for plant growth and might in the long run save the farmer from the curse of insecticides and weed killers. My spacetime-light movement, double-photon experiment will, without question, lead to our understanding of fast growth (cancer). If so, my love of Mary will have paid big dividends. I myself may never get worldly honor for that discovery, but that is of little importance if, upon my death, the Virgin Mary is present to meet me at God's great doorway.

Footnotes

Chapter I — Outside the Kitchen Door

1. Small songbird species often fly against windowpanes. There is no good explanation for this behavior except the rather simplified one that they are attacking their own image in the belief that it is a strange bird coveting their territory. Males are territorial but female are not, so that does not answer why it is as likely to be a female as a male. "Bird Banding," *National Geographic*, Dec. 1928.

2. When I was a boy, all the articles in the then marvelous *National Geographic* were written by freelance individuals who were experts on subjects like bird banding, or had unique hobbies such as falconry. Today it has degenerated into a slick coffee-table journal with articles written by staff reporters. Thus has modern school journalism gained control of publishing, and driven it to a dull linearity and monotonous style.

3. Many modern anthropologists and archeologists refute the common belief that man evolved from a hunting species, that is by killing larger animals for food. All the evidence points to the fact that early man was a food gatherer, and that his main source of protein was insects. The Air Force pilot who was shot down over Bosnia survived in just that manner.

4. "Falconry, The Sport of Kings," *National Geographic*, December, 1920. By far the best article ever written on falconry.

Chapter II — A Hawk for the Bush

1. Today it is illegal to keep any wild bird, even a magpie or crow, as a pet. These rules are applied with such rigid control that people have been fined for trying to feed and save an injured wild bird. Admittedly, most wild birds do not make good pets; certain ones like magpies, crows and starlings (which farmers can still legally kill) make excellent pets and are unequaled as a means for teaching the young responsibility and love of nature.

2. *Keenness* is a term not found in the glossary of most books on falconry, but is commonly used by practicing falconers to mean a hawk or falcon "keen" to hunt — that is, a slightly hungry bird. Critics will say falconers starve their birds. This is not true. For a human to wish dinner, he or she must first feel hungry. A hawk that is "fed up," as a falconer will say, will fly off and sit in a tree and, eventually, be lost.

It is simple to determine when a trained falcon is "keen" by keeping track of its average weight. There is an optimum weight at which a bird of prey is hungry but not starved. In other words, a falcon controls when its master can utilize it in the hunt.

3. Most birds of prey, even eagles, will not attack a human being at the nest. The one exception is the members of the short-winged, woods hunting hawks of the family Accipiteridae. The group in the U.S. includes the little sharp-shinned hawk, mid-sized Cooper's hawk, and large, fierce goshawk. Falcons, like the peregrine and kestrel, have long, pointed wings for open-space hunting, and the accipiter has short, rounded wings for flying between trees and bushes.

Chapter III — Radioman

1. C47s were the transport workhorses of the Army Air Corps in World War II. They were the military version of the old commercial DC3. Not only were they utilized by Air Transport Command (ATC) for supplies, they were the main aircraft of Troop Carrier Command, and dropped paratroopers, including my brother Eugene, out across the battlefields of Europe.

2. Our parish priest, Father Michael Williams, in a homily one Sunday talked about how he once had the exact same feeling of joy. It occurred while driving his car on a stormy night along the Florida coast near Jacksonville. It also occurred to him at an unusual time of his life, as it had with me. He had been ordained in Rome shortly before. Until Father Michael spoke, I thought such occurrences were a part of my character alone.

3. Almost all of the B17s of the 8th Air Force Bomber Command came to England across the Arctic. Between Great Falls, Montana, their point of departure, and the last beam station in Ireland, were a series of Arctic and Icelander beam (radio range) stations. Most of the B17s overflew Stornoway, Scotland to Prestwick, Scotland. Ones that strayed south came over Belleek. The big C54 Air Transport Command aircraft came straight across from Newfoundland to Belleek, Ireland

The other use of the American station was to guide the Coastal Command RAF flying boats, in bad weather, to Lough Erne for a safe landing.

Chapter IV — On the Border

1. Belleek, although a very small village, is renowned for its famous Belleek pottery. It is considered among the finest delicate parian in the world. Its trademark of harp and Irish wolfhound at the base of a round tower, is well known around the world.

2. I was saddened when, in Tokyo, I received a letter from Marty's brother Tom saying that Marty died on the operating table while undergoing a new "cure" for asthma. I had left Ireland two years before. The seminary would not accept Marty with asthma.

3. See *Spies in Ireland*, Macdonald & Co., Ltd. England, 1963. (Originally published in German as *Geheimauftag Irland*, Hamburg, 1961).

4. In 1984 I hired an RAF historian in London to track down the original RAF warning to our station. The place mentioned was Belleek and the code word PhilC. The official message also included a short notice that the poet Brendan Beehan was being deported to Ireland for IRA activities in England.

Chapter V — Some Unsolved Mysteries

1. It is said that Frank S. Baum came upon the name, *Land of Oz*, while making the story up for his children. He glanced up at his file cabinet and noted the last drawer went from O to Z — Oz.

2. The Grand Canal, which was built in 1772 by The Grand Canal Company, links Dublin with the Barrow and Shannon rivers. It winds through the beautiful midlands of Ireland to Robertstown, Tullamore and Banagher to Shannon Harbor. It fell into disuse after World War II, but was restored for small-craft traffic in the 1980s. My son and I hiked the length of the tow path during the summer of 1978. The long hike is recorded in the March-April (1979) issue of *Ireland of the Welcomes*, published by Bord Failte (The Irish Tourist Board).

3. The history of Lough Derg has been documented by the school master of Belleek, John B. Cunningham. *Lough Derg, Legendary Pilgrimage*, (Monagh, 1984).

Chapter VI — Leper's Rock

1. The diary of my journey around the world was published in 1988 by *Acres U.S.A.* under the title, *A Walk in the Sun.*

2. See *What Catholics Believe About Mary*, By Rev. Peter M. J. Stravinskas, Our Sunday Visitor Inc. Publ., Huntington, Indiana, 1988.

Chapter VII — Form and Frequency

1. Thomas Merton, *New Seeds of Contemplation*, A New Direction Book, Abby of Gethsemani, Inc., Kentucky, 1961.

2. The two long appendages that one sees on the heads of insects are only the support, with the nerve path, from which the real antennae, microscopic spines called sensilla, emerge. There are over 300 different shaped sensilla and pits (antennae and resonant cavities) on different insects. They are not coated with metal but with an insulative semiconductor substance — wax. Electrical engineers would call them open resonator, dielectric (insulative) arrays.

3. The sperm sack is shaped like a bulb with a long neck on it. A hook at the end holds it in place at the entrance of the female sperm tube. It resembles a plastic structure, and is inserted, over an hour-long period, into a female storage organ called a *bursa copulatrix*. The number of stored sacs equals the number of matings.

4. I had no sooner finished my antenna work when the scanning electron microscope was invented. I obtained one of the first ever produced by the Cambridge, England company, and rechecked my long years of work in fifteen days — there was not a single error. Those difficult days of histology and morphology are forgotten now, and modern researchers demonstrate a concealed sort of contempt for such work, they would, however, be lost without their sophisticated technical instruments.

5. I later was the first to write a long paper describing the many different types of sensilla.

6. In laser physics this is called "pumping" the energy up to a higher level in the atom so that when it falls back to ground state it emits photons of infrared radiation or light.

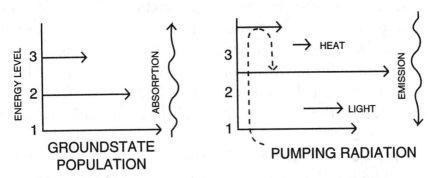

7. Scatter radiation is caused by collisions of atoms or molecules with each other or against special etched surfaces such as are found on insect antenna.

8. See list of author's scientific papers in the appendix.

9. The award reads "for theories of insect communication by infrared and microwave." It should have said by *infrared and ELF radio.*

Chapter VIII — The Virgin and the Magpie

1. See Appendix II for candle paper (1977).

2. I have asked many women if, on a romantic evening out, they would prefer light bulbs or candles on the dining table. All have answered candles. Some churches have replaced candles with with light bulbs. I suspect a poll of worshipers would give the same totality in favor of candles.

3. I never had a pet magpie that mimicked a single word. My parrots all have been able to mimic words.

4. That fact alone mediated against us ever getting close to the sacred image.

5. See Appendix II for UFO paper (1979).

6. I have been unable to find out exactly when the beautiful frescoes were added to the chapel wall, but was told by one priest it was in the '40s.

7. Historians of falconry agree that it was never a sport in Mexico.

8. No apparition has ever been sanctioned by an English-speaking bishop (Irish, English or American). The Irish will speak of Knock, but it has never received a bishop's sanction — a requirement for recognition. Latin, French, and Asiatic bishops have sanctioned hundreds of such little miracles. It is further proof of the skeptical materialism of English-speaking, Western society.

Chapter IX — Divine Providence

1. The Rev. Father de Ravignan first had the inspiration to erect a statue of Mary on the Roche Cornelle. Four years later, Father Combolot, Monsignor de Morlhon, Bishop of Le Puy began the project. A statue of the good bishop was cast and placed at the foot of the larger statue of Mary.

2. It is on the black stone that sick pilgrims come to ask the Virgin to heal them. It has been so since the early history of Le Puy.

3. Le Puy as a place of pilgrimage predates all these 19th and 20th-century sites by over a thousand years. It is known that the town has been renown as an apparition site since the middle of the 9th century. The first crusade, began by Peter the Hermit, started from Le Puy. Thirteen kings of France and a whole line of popes, beginning with Urban II, visited the site. Charlemagne is said to have visited it, as did Joan of Arc's mother in 1429. The holy image in the Moorish-looking Cathedral is known as the Black Virgin, and is believed to be given to the people of Le Puy by Saint Louis the King.

4. Taken from Andre Chanal's little pamphlet, *Le Puy*, Xavier Mappus, 52 Ave. Foch, Le Puy, France.

5. I first began to study the effect of tall stone structures (stone antenna) on plants at Devenish Island, Ireland. I noticed the grass around the tower was more green and lush than elsewhere. (See my book, *Paramagnetism*.)

6. During World War II Normoyle was one of the biggest army motor ordinance bases in the United States. Before going into the Army Air Force, I worked as a requisition messenger on the base.

Chapter X — Paintbox Explorer

1. Winsor Newton makes a small, pocket-size watercolor kit that contains a water bottle, brushes and mixing pallets. It is very convenient for travel.

2. The best book on Divine Providence is the one written by Jean-Pierre De Caussade, S.J. It is called *Abandonment to Divine Providence*, Doubleday Books, 1975. It was not published until long after his death in 1751. It consists of letters on spiritual subjects to the nuns of a convent.

3. See my book, *Paramagnetism — Rediscovering Nature's Secret Force of Growth*, Acres U.S.A., 1995.

4. In my laboratory, I would put a few drops of ammonia on a piece of cotton near a scent I was looking at with my Fourier transform spectrophotometer. Invariably the infrared lines (frequencies being emitted) as I flowed the scent would increase in amplitude (height on recorder). Sometimes they would also shift slightly to longer infrared wavelegths.

5. Before I left I discovered that the Egyptians blamed the Russians for the dam, and wished they had never built such a huge structure, but instead many controllable smaller power stations.

6. Paramagnetism (rock & soil) and diamagnetism (plants) are obviously the yang (male) and yin (female) of the Chinese.

7. I took two photos (because it was dusk) to bracket the exposure. The first one (slow) showed nothing, the second

one, taken at a faster speed, showed the "laser lines." My friend Jerry Hale, of Gainesville, was taping with me using his video camera. The recorder showed no light coming from the windows. They were totally dark.

Chapter XI — Holographic Rocks

1. M. Scott Peck, M.D., *In Search of Stones*, Hyperion, New York, 1988. A beautifully written book about a husband and wife's adventures among the ancient stone structures of England and Scotland.

2. I believe that the further destruction of the envirorn-ment, for instance by weakening the Environmental Protection Agency, is the greatest danger that civilization faces today. The destruction of humans (abortion), the destruction of nature (God's creation) by greed, and uncaring harvesting of resources is exactly what Mary is warning us about.

Chapter XII — Laser Light from God

1. I have talked to quite a few priests and bishops and get the same answer. Mary distracts our thoughts from the cross. I ask again why — or better yet, how?

2. Geiger counters register photons of gamma radiation by counting each single photon strike on the detector face.

3. There is little difference between the way the Achuara tribe live and farm in their thatched-roofed village, and the way the rural folks of the Irish countryside live and farm in and around their little country thatched roofed villages. Anthropologists always emphasize the details of differences when they should be concentrating on the sameness of these nature-compatible life styles. The Irish country people even prayed and healed the same way — to one God and through lots of different spirit helpers (saints). I should know since I lived in what might be called 19th-century Ireland (1944-46), and with the Achuara as the first white man during quite a few months between 1992-94. I had nothing to prove about these

people's lives, as in Ireland, I was keeping track of manmade ELF radio waves (aircraft), and in the Amazon measuring natural ELF (atmospheric) radio waves. Because the Irish have political rebels, and the Achuara a few mafia (head shrinking squads), proves no more about these people than the Montana ranch terrorists prove about Americans. They are small pockets of devil-controlled humans — prayer will defeat them.

4. If you had enough hours in the air in propeller aircraft, you soon learn when the platform is about to drop by stalling out. Just before a stall you can sense a slight quiver in the aircraft — almost like a little mechanical gasp. It didn't happen.

APPENDIX I
Spacetime as a Sine Wave

The wave theory of light was postulated by Robert Hooke and C. Huygens in the 17th century. Although the wave theory was accepted by most, it is well known that Isaac Newton, in contrast, favored a particle theory. He believed that light went forth as little "particles" of energy, or "corpuscles" of energy. This became known as the corpuscular theory of light. Newton also believed in an absolute fixed time (Hawkins, 1988). In his first thesis he was close to correct as we now utilize both wave and corpuscular theory (quantum mechanics) to describe light. His second thesis was proved wrong by Albert Einstein in 1906.

Wave theory works very well for radio antenna design and quantum theory for lasers.

My long interest in the well known phenomenon of a moth's attraction to candles, and also in Einstein's studies on thermodynamic non-equilibrium in space (cavity resonance) led directly to these experiments.

Insect sensilla (spines on antenna) are most certainly analogous to spatial resonant cavities in that they are designed as an open resonator dielectric waveguide. Since insect antenna are separated slightly on the head and duplicate morphologically one another, they also form a stereoscopic system, two intensities separated by a small distance. In this they resemble our own eyes.

Almost any surface in nature must, some place in the electromagnetic spectrum, "emit" coherent scatter which can be resonated by such a dielectric spine system. This makes the field of surface morphology extremely important to any understanding of how nature operates, e.g. surface of skin, surface of a leaf or indeed the surface of a flame. See patent No. 5,424,551 *Frequency Emitter for control of Insects* (Callahan, 1996).

THE INTENSITY INTERFEROMETER

There are numerous types of spectrophotometers for the study of photon emission and absorption. Unfortunately none sold for laboratory work are really suitable for the detection of very low energy scatter radiation at various angles.

The most sensitive are the Fourier Transform type designed mainly for absorption work by chemists. During my studies of insect scents (semiochemicals) I began in 1969 to utilize a modified (by me) Digilab Fourier Transform System. I discovered that photo scatter from the atmosphere scent "plasma," into which the insect inserted its antenna, could be made coherent by utilizing different hairy or reticulated surfaces as scatter plates. The insects decode these coherent scatter lines with their dielectric waveguide spines — in short, olfaction is wavelength-photon mediated.

Many different types of infrared and spectrophotometers are described in books on radio astronomy.

One such book is *The Exploration of Space by Radio*, written by Hanbury Brown and Sir Bernard Lovell (1957).

Unfortunately, this book does not describe the astute contribution that Hanbury Brown and Twiss made to astronomy, and to the study of the statistical properties of radio and visible light with their invention of the intensity interferometer (see the review by Bertolotti, 1983).

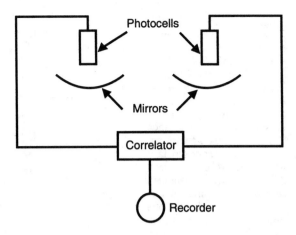

Fig. 1

The intensity spectrophotometer is essentially a modification of the two antenna radio telescope. It also resembles, in considerable detail, the four-element American navigation radio range system of World War II and the German two-element system. This type of interferometer is designed to correlate the intensity of light, or radio, from two different point sources of photon emission. It is also utilized to calculate the separation between stars. Hanbury Brown and Twiss modified their radio version in order to study light under laboratory conditions.

They reported in 1957 that light beams of narrow spectral width have a "tendency" to arrive at detectors in correlated pairs. This thesis, of course, elicited considerable controversy between physicist and the astronomers. The physicists were quite certain, based on studies by Adam, Janossy and Varga, (1955) quoted in translation from Bertolotti, that there is no correlation whatsoever between photons pulses provided in two separate detectors illuminated by a single coherent light.

According to their interpretation of quantum theory, photons should arrive at the detector surfaces independent of one another. However, in my youth when photographing bird nests closeup, I often wondered why successive negatives, at their edge, from closeup photos "bracketed," by shots taken in dim woods and at different speeds, showed shifts between negatives at their edge — that is, space shifts through shutter speed.

The Hanbury Brown-Twiss intensity interferometer, in essence, consists of two photocells (antenna) and focusing mirrors. The energy from a single source (or two sources) is picked up by the cells and fed into a correlator and recorder (Fig. 1).

The correlator counts the photon hits and determines how many arrive at the same time. This system is of course the same as my World War II radio range (call code Belleek) low frequency system.

Two towers are fed in phase at one time by an A signal (- —) and two at right angles by an N (— -). Where the field figure patterns overlap there is a steady tone (Fig. 2).

The intensity spectrophotometer is, of course, a receiver, and the radio range a transmitter, but the reciprocal law states that any system that is a good transmitting antenna is also a good receiving antenna.

The two towers A, along with two towers N, were fed from a single transmitter (source) and tuned by feeder lines to resonate, but each pair (A & N) was keyed at a totally separate time! This means that when the figure 8 pattern of A was on, N was off. Yet where A & N patterns overlap there is a steady tone. Since one is dealing with waves almost a kilometer long how can this be? The AN figure 8 patterns are 100% out of time phase? Remember there is only one transmitter (single source) feeding towers out of time

Perhaps the photons from towers A catch up with those from towers N at the receiver antenna.

If one considers two race horses confined to a track and one overtakes the other, then there is one instant when they are next to each other and space and time are correlated. In other words they are in one plain at one time. Once racehorse A passes B, he is moving faster than the steady pace of B. In order to photograph both horses from the side as one (one obscuring the other, paired) the photograph would have to be accurately timed so that they were both in the same plane. Remember, however, if the track was curved and A was traveling the speed of light, B could catch up (shorter distance) on the inside without going faster than A (the speed of light), In other words, perhaps time is curved, or time and space, as Einstein theorized, are curved.

The experiments that originally proved the dual quality of wave and particle theory utilized an electron beam to form diffraction circles on a screen (like a rock produces water waves). They are called Airy's rings (after the great 17th century scientist). They are so well known that they need no detailed description. In summary, a phosphor screen shows both waves (Airy's rings) and little particles (quantum) scattered on its surface from the electron gun.

My work with multiplicative antenna long ago convinced me that a simple roll of 35mm color film is not only a large flat plane, multicative aerial for photon detection, but also the perfect detector for a study utilizing the concept of intensity interferometery. This should be obvious since film is a thin layer, solid state (large angle) photon detection intensity system. It is of course also a very cheap photon detector.

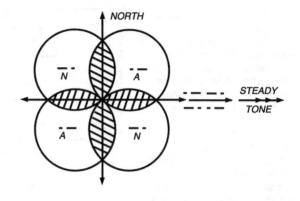

BELLEEK'S MODULATED RADIO RANGE

Fig. 2

METHODS

The first photographs of laser emission I obtained were preliminary experiments to see if I could obtain Airy's defraction patterns from a laser, with straight lines, of course — the same as the ones obtained on my eye surface by squinting with partially closed lids at the sun or a candle. Although the camera was on a tripod and the laser on a stack of books, I did not anticipate any alignment problems. However, as I expected, my first laser images were not centered on the film. For a moment I thought parallax, but quickly realized I was using my Nikon FM2 single lens reflex and not a viewfinder camera. My second thought was that I had hit the books sending the laser beam at an angle to the camera (despite my expectation of a space jump due to my boyhood bird pictures).

I next constructed an optical bench out of two pieces of heavy oak wood at right angles to each other. I mounted the camera with C clamps at one end and a helium neon (pointer laser) at the opposite. Both were on ball and socket joints so that fine adjustments could be made. I also mounted a ball and socket platform between the laser and camera for my candle.

Since the camera lens tended to scatter and reflect some of the laser energy, making measurements difficult, I turned my FM2 Nikon into a pinhole camera. It thus becomes the same type of (electron gun)

photon-pinhole lens-screen system as that used originally to show wave and quantum energy by means of Airy's diffraction rings and dots on the phosphor screen.

The pinhole camera was constructed by the simple means of taking the lens off the camera body and replacing it with a body cap made by Nikon for protecting the body opening. In the center of the cap I drilled a 2-mm hole equal to a camera aperture of f 16 on the camera lens. I could also cover this larger hole with black paper punched with a pin equal to the aperture of ca f 128 (extremely small).

The Nikon FM2 has a horizontal focal-plane shutter with speeds from bulb (timed) through 1 sec. and up to 1/4000 sec. It is an extremely well made instrument with accurate shutter speeds.

I proceeded to take a long series of photographs at speeds of 25 seconds, 20,15, 10, 5, 1, 1/2, 1/4, 1/8, 1/15, 1/30, etc., up to 1/4000. The optimal range for study and usable light intensity lay between 5 sec. and 1/30 sec., so that the most of the data analyzed cover this time range.

As I suspected from my first photographs, the figure of the laser beam, although fixed in place, moved with shutter speed (time). I was obtaining once again image movement by varying shutter speeds, only now instead of youthful bird photographs I was using controlled laser energy photon photographs. I also obtained, as I knew I would, the mystic Airy's rings and the parallel lines observed by the astute Pueblo Indians.

Since (Hanbury Brown and Twiss, 1957) the intensity spectrophotometer was utilized on starlight (incoherent sources) I utilized a regular 75W light bulb, candle and flashlight, in addition to the coherent helium-neon laser.

A friend suggested that the image movements (by time) were caused either by parallex, an impossibility for a single pinhole system and reflex camera, or by the shutter slit of the focal plane shutter. The Nikon shutter goes from top to bottom, and not side to side, as in many cameras. This also seemed to me an impossibility, nevertheless I ran a check with a Rolli 35 camera, which has a centered lens with a round leaf aperture.

The camera, laser and candle were always aligned accurately by pointing the laser at the center split image range finder (without the pinhole lens cap) and observing the two spots (split image) on a white card behind the viewfinder. The lens cap was then placed over the camera opening and a pin hole punched into the black paper over the hole exactly in the center of the laser beam. This assured a near perfect alignment.

All recordings were measured from the right edge of the film print to the center of the laser or on the wick of the candle (since flames move).

In all I used 20 rolls of 400-speed Fuji color film for a total of 720 photos. In all cases the image, though centered perfectly, moved with time.

RESULTS

The results of these experiments on time and space are given in figures 3A-F.

Fig. 3A is one run of a 75W tungsten light bulb from gooseneck lamp pressed directly against the pin hole. The distance between the hot radiation source and the camera pin hole is only the paper thin edge of the black paper pin hole. It will be noted that from 1 to 1/60 sec. the curve is flat (no pin hole focus).

Fig. 3B is a curve from a flashlight (two battery type) positioned 4 cm from the pin hole (focused).

Fig. 3C and Fig. 3E are comparisons of curves from two beams, candle and laser,with the candle 4 cm. in the distance. The laser beam was centered on the candle flame at a distance of 8 cm. behind it.

Fig. 3D is the laser beam by itself from 1 sec. to 1/60 sec. The curve usually changes at ca. 1/30 sec.

Fig. 3F is a comparison of the candle with the laser beam placed to the side of the candle. Note that the curves follow each other but at times they separate eg. 1/2 and 1/4 sec.

Since the laser beam is narrow band over such distances the distance position of the laser behind the candle flame is not significant over such short distances.

In all cases (5 in all) where the candle flame was close to the pin hole (4 cm. in distance) an almost perfect sign wave was plotted (Figs. 3C & 3E).

DISCUSSION AND CONCLUSION

Physicists and astronomers that study the Universe use a model based on a double cone. One cone represents the future, the other the past, and where they are joined, the present.

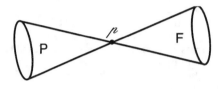

A cosmic section (cone), as is well known from solid geometry, is defined as a set of points such as the distance from a fixed point divided by the distance from a fixed line is a constant. The fixed point of course is the focus (x) *e.g.* surface of a three layered film, and the fixed line, the directrix or y axis.

The "fit" of this directrix through the two cones and the plot of the points forms a parabola (standing wave). Time of course, as in any "radio" system moves. In such a plot e is called the eccentricity (e = 1).

As is well understood, if e ≠ 1, then: it should be possible to use the equation for the standing wave (parabola) since e = 1 is the definition of a parabola (moving) or standing) where:

$$\frac{\sqrt{(x-p)^2+y^2}}{x} = E$$

Working through said definition one ends up with:

$$\frac{(x-h)^2}{a^2} + \frac{y^2}{B} = 1 \text{ then } B = \frac{e^2p^2}{1-e^2}$$

If e is greater (e>1) then one B is negative; less one B is positive (e<1).

Thus + would be the observable image and - would be the invisible image below ground level.

We may now understand, See Fig. 4, how the + parts carries the "off center"

image, and the displaced recursive part below carries the unseen ground wave image.

The most obvious and irrefutable conclusion of this work is that there is a detector surface time sine wave. Although the work of Einstein demonstrated that space is curved, neither Einstein's work nor the work of Handbury Brown and Twiss (1967) ever suggested that time, at a detector surface, formed "itself" into a sine wave. It is, of course, obvious that if an electron correlator is used, as in the Handbury Brown and Twiss experiments, this phenomenon could not be demonstrated. It was discovered utilizing film as an intensity interferometer. The sine wave character of time is very distinctly illustrated figures 3 A to F.

This experiment is repeatable with a minimum of expense, *e.g.* a reflex camera, candle and laser pointer — inexpensive

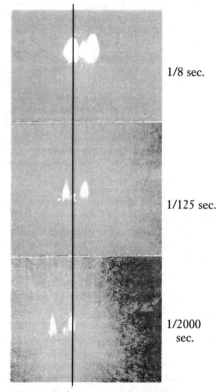

1/8 sec.

1/125 sec.

1/2000 sec.

Fig. 5 — Double image and movement with time.

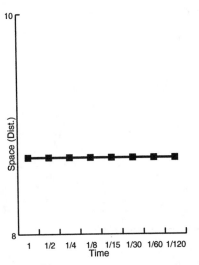

Fig. 3A

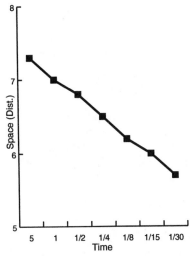

Fig. 3B

items. Despite the simplicity of the experiments it is easily understandable that the results of these experiments have considerable significience to our understanding of nature, communication systems and even mysticism as it is understood presently.

A close look at the laser energy imprinted on the film demonstrates both particles (quantum theory) and Airy's rings (wave theory). In short, it is a second proof of wave-quantum duality, however, that these particles are not evident in an incoherent flashlight experiments.

The theory of the brain as a holographic system (Penfield, 1975) is well known and discussed beautifully in the book *The Holographic Universe* (1991) by Michael Talbot. The simple fact that the brain is bilobed and that coherence is a part of living systems (Callahan, 1965, 1967 and 1989) and Popp, Li and Gu (1992) lends excellent support to the brain functioning as a holographic system, this work strongly supports the Penfield theory in as much as two synchronized photons are needed to form a holographic information (bit) storage system in a brain.

It is strange that in all of present day intensity work, the equally elegant work of the astronomers Handbury Brown and

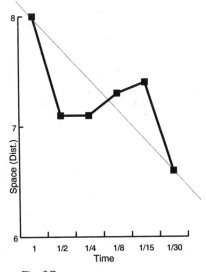

Fig. 3C

Twiss, and their intensity interferometer, should have been overlooked.

Finally and most importantly the offset of images occur because two points on any sine wave are 180° out of phase (+ and -), as one is up the opposite is down. In short there is one film image visible (+) and an opposite second invisible image (-) at the

Appendix I   189

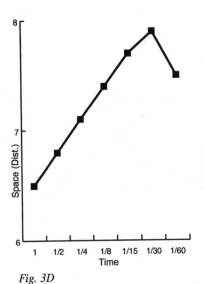

Fig. 3D

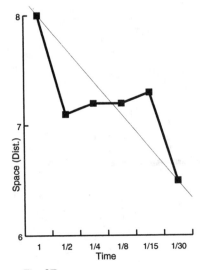

Fig. 3E

other side of the center line of the film. The fact that the two images, (of the double image), are not exact reflections indicates that double images only occur when the steep sine wave is crossing near the bottom base line, which is 0 point (Fig. 4 & 5). If my reader looks closely at Fig. 5, he or she will note that the right candle flame and laser beam are slightly larger and differently

shaped than the left indicating not a mirror image, but instead a second image caught after a split second change at the 0 crossover in space of the time domain.

The fact that there is a double visible image at the base line of the time sine wave, and that at other periods of ridges and valleys a visible (+) and in all likelihood an opposite (-) invisible image exists, and that

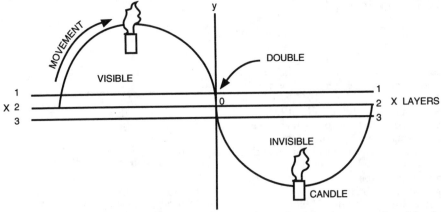

Fig. 4. The bending and moving is not, of course, due to the refraction properties of the three layers, e.g. film, or plant leaf, and in accordance to Snell's law, since it reverses itself 180 degrees.

190 *My Search for Traces of God*

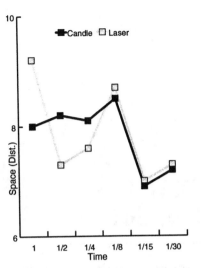

Fig. 3F

in all probability the brain works as a holographic system, opens up so many doors for the ghosts and apparitions of the mystic life as to stagger the imagination.

In conclusions the main summary of the work are:

1. Time at a detector surface is a sine wave (goes + & -)

2. When an incoherent (DC battery) source is compared to a coherent source the incoherent source usually demonstrates a flatter sine wave curve.

3. When coherent and incoherent source are together, on the same run, the curves are similar and at certain times the spacing of side to side sources change.

4. It is possible to obtain a double image at times, indicating that this is a double photon phenomenon (paired at the detector).

LITERATURE CITED

1. Adam, A., J. Janossy & P. Varga. (1955). *Acta. Phys. Hung.* 4:301. Quoted from Bertolotti (*Masers & Lasers*, 1983). Adam Hilger Ltd. Bristol.
2. Callahan, P. S. (1965). *Annals. Ent. Soc. Amer.* 58:727-745.
3. Callahan, P .S. (1967). Misc. Pub. *Ent. Soc. Amer.* 5 (7) 315-347.
4. Callahan P. S. (1989). *Medical Hypothesis.* 28:99-105.
5. Handbury Brown, R. & B. Lovell (1957). *The Exploration of Space*, Chapman & Hall, Ltd. London.
6. Handbury Brown, R & Q. Twiss (1957). *Nature.* 179: 1128.
7. Hawkins, S. W. (1988). *A Brief History of Time.* Bantam Books. N. Y.
8. Penfield, Wilder, (1975). *The Mystery of the Mind.* Princeton Univ. Press. Princeton, N.J.
9. Popp, F. A., K.H. Li & Q. Gu. (1992) *Biophoton Research.* World Scientific Press. London.
10. Talbot, Michael, (1991). "The Holographic Universe." *Harper Perennial.* New York.

APPENDIX II
Author's Publications

Papers:

Callahan, P.S. and H. Young (1955). "Observations on the avifauna of an Ozark plateau." *Auk.* 72: 267-78.

Callahan, P.S. (1957). "Oviposition response of the corn earworm to differences in surface texture." *J. Kan. Ent. Soc.* 30:59-63.

Callahan, P.S. (1957). "Oviposition response of the imago of the corn earworm *Heliothis zea* (Boddie), to various wavelengths of light." *Ann. Entomol. Soc. Amer.* 50(5): 444-452.

Callahan, P.S. (1958). "Behavior of the imago of the corn earworm, *Heliothis zea* (Boddie), with special reference to emergence and reproduction." *Ann. Entomol. Soc. Am.* 51: 271 -283.

Callahan, P.S. (1958). "Serial morphology as a technique for determination of reproductive patterns in the corn earworm, *Heliothis zea* (Boddie)." *Ann. Entomol. Soc. Am.* 51: 413-428.

Callahan, P.S. (1958). "The strawberry sap beetle, *Lobiopa insularis.*" *Insect Conditions in Louisiana.* pp. 14- 15.

Callahan, P.S. (1958). "Survey of cutworms affecting truck crops." *Insect Conditions in Louisiana.* pp. 16-18.

Blum, M.S., J.R. Walker, and P.S. Callahan (1958). "Chemical insecticidal, and antibiotic properties of fire ant venom." *Science,* 128: 306-307.

Callahan, P. S., M.S. Blum, and J.R. Walker (1959). "Morphology and histology of the poison glands and sting of the imported fire ant (*Solenopsis saevissima v.* Richter Forel)." *Ann. Entomol. Soc. Am.* 52: 573-590.

Callahan, P.S. and J.B. Chapin (1959). "Economic moth populations in the Baton Rouge area." *Insect Conditions in Louisiana.* pp. 46-48.

Callahan, P.S., R. Brown, and A. Dearman (1960). "Control of tomato insect pests in Louisiana." *Louisiana Agriculture* 3: 1 -3.

Callahan, P.S. and J.B. Chapin (1960). "Morphology of the reproductive systems and mating in two representatives members of the family Noctuidae, *Pseudaletia unipuncta* (Haw.) and *Peridroma margaritosa* (Haw.) with comparison to *Heliothis zea* (Boddie)." *Ann. Entomol. Soc. Am.* 53: 763-782.

Callahan, P.S. and J.B. Chapin (1960). "Economic moth populations in the Baton Rouge area for 1960." *Insect Conditions in Louisiana.* pp. 46-47.

Callahan, P.S. (1961). "Relationship of the crop capacity to the depletion of the fat body and egg development in the corn earworm, *Heliothis zea,* and the fall armyworm, *Laphygma frugiperda* (Lepidoptera: Noctuidae)." *Ann. Entomol. Soc. Am.* 54: 819-827.

Callahan, P.S. (1962). "Techniques for rearing the corn earworm, *Heliothis zea* (Boddie)." *J. Econ. Entomol.* 55: 453457.

Blum, M.S. and P. S. Callahan (1963). "The venom and poison glands of *Pseudomyrmex pallidus* (F. Smith)." *Phyche* 70: 70-74.

Callahan, P.S. and T. Cascio (1963). "Histology of the reproductive tracts and transmission of sperm in the corn earworm, *Heliothis zea.*" *Ann. Entomol. Soc. Am.* 56: 535-556.

Callahan, P.S. (1964). "An inexpensive actinometer for continuous field recording of moonlight, daylight, or low intensity evening light." *J. Econ. Entomol.* 57: 758-760.

Callahan, P.S. (1964). "Basic semiconductor circuitry for ecological and behavioral studies of insects." *ARS* 33-94.

Callahan, P.S. (1965). "Intermediate and far infrared sensing of nocturnal insects. Part I. Evidences for a far infrared (FIR) electromagnetic theory of communication and sensing in moths and its relationship to the limiting biosphere of the corn earworm, *Heliothis zea*." *Ann. Entomol. Soc. Am.* 58: 727-745.

Callahan, P.S. (1965). "Intermediate and far infrared sensing of nocturnal insects. Part II. The compound eye of the corn earworm, *Heliothis zea*, and other moths as a mosaic optic-electromagnetic thermal radiometer." *Ann Entomol. Soc. Am.* 58: 746-756.

Callahan, P.S. (1965). "An infrared electromagnetic theory of diapause inducement and control in insects." *Ann. Entomol. Soc. Am.* 58: 561-564.

Callahan, P.S. (1965). "Far infrared emission and detection by night flying moths." *Nature*, 207: 1172-1173.

Callahan, P.S. (1965). "A photoelectric-photographic analysis of flight behavior in the corn earworm, *Heliothis zea*, and other moths." *Ann. Entomol. Soc. Am.* 58: 159-169.

Callahan, P.S. (1966). "Do insects communicate by radio?" *Animals*, 8: 197-201.

Callahan, P.S. (1966). "Electromagnetic communication in insects . . . elements of the terrestrial infrared environment, including generation, transmission, and detection by moths." *ARS* 33-110. pp. 156-176.

Callahan, P.S. (1966). "Infrared stimulation of nocturnal moths." *J. Ga. Ent. Soc.* I: 6-14.

Callahan, P.S. and A.R. Chauthani (1966). "A method for repointing insect dissecting forceps." *J. Econ. Entomol.* 59: 490-491.

Chauthani, A.R. and P.S. Callahan (1966). "A dissection technique for studying internal anatomy of different stadia of Noctuidae." *Ann. Entomol. Soc. Am.* 59: 1017-1018.

Valli, V.J. and P.S. Callahan (1966). "Biometeorological fluctuations affecting the ecology of *Heliothis zea* I." *Ga. Coastal Plain Exp. Sta. Mimeograph* Ser. N.S. 248, 11 pp.

Starks, K.J., P.S. Callahan, W.W. McMillian, and H.C. Cox (1966). "A photoelectric counter to monitor olfactory response in moths." *J. Econ. Entomol.* 59: 1015-1016.

Callahan, P.S. (1967). "Insect molecular bioelectronics: a theoretical and experimental study of insect sensillae as tubular waveguides, with particular emphasis on their dielectric and thermoelectret properties." *Misc. Public. Entomol. Soc. Amer.* 5(7): 315-347.

Snow, J.W. and P.S. Callahan (1967). "Laboratory mating studies of the corn earworm, *Heliothis zea* (Lepidoptera: Noctuidae)." *Ann. Entomol. Soc. Am.* 60: 1066-1071.

Chautharni, A.R. and P.S. Callahan (1967). "The nervous system of the corn earworm moth, *Heliothis zea* (Lepidoptera: Noctuidae)." *Ann. Entomol. Soc. Am.* 60: 248-255.

Chauthani, A.R. and P.S. Callahan (1967). "Developmental morphology of the alimentary canal of *Heliothis zea* (Lepidoptera: Noctuidae)." *Ann. Entomol. Soc. Am.* 60: 1136-1141.

Chauthani, A.R. and P.S. Callahan (1967). "A comparison of the larval and pupal nervous systems of the corn earworm, *Heliothis zea* (Lepidoptera: Noctuidae)." *Ann. Entomol. Soc. Am.* 60:1141-1 146.

Callahan, P. S. (1968). "A high frequency dielectric waveguide on the antennae of night-flying moths (Saturnidae)." *J. Appl. Optics* 7: 1425-1430.

Callahan, P.S. (1968). "Nondestructive temperature and radiance measurements on night-flying moths." *J. Appl. Optics* 7: 1811-1817.

Manghum, C.L. and P.S. Callahan (1968). "Attraction of near-infrared radiation to *Aedes aegypti.*" *J. Econ. Entomol.* 61: 36-37.

Callahan, P.S., E.F. Taschenberg, and T. Carlysle (1968). "The scape and pedicel dome sensors — a dielectric aerial waveguide on the antennae of the night-flying moths." *Ann. Entomol. Soc. Am.* 61: 934-937.

Snow, J.W. and P.S. Callahan (1968). "Biological and morphological studies of the granulate cutworm, *Feltia subterranea* (F.) in Georgia and Louisiana." *Ga. Agri. Res. Bull.* No. 42, 23 pp.

Valli, V.J. and P.S. Callahan (1968). "The effect of bioclimate on the communication system of night-flying moths." *Inter. J. Biomet.* 12: 99-118.

Callahan, P.S. (1969). Section, "infrared research," in chapter "Physical and mechanical control." *Principles of Insect Pest Management.* J.V. Osmun (ed.). *Natl. Acad. Sci.*, Wash, D.C. p. 508.

Callahan, P.S. (1970). "Evolution, ecology, and enforcement." *Assoc. Food & Drug Officials* U.S. 34(4): 227-232.

Callahan, P.S. and L. Goldman (1970). "Response of *Aedes aegypti* to 10.6 micron radiation." *First Quarterly Report*, Insect Attractants, Behavior, and Basic Biology Research Laboratory, Gainesville, Florida.

Callahan, P.S. (1971). "Far infrared stimulation of insects with the *Glagolewa-arkadiewa* 'mass radiator.'" *Fla. Entomol.* 54(2): 201-204.

Callahan, P.S. and T.C. Carlysle (1971). "A function of the epiphysis on the foreleg of the corn earworm moth, *Heliothis zea.*" *Ann. Entomol. Soc. Amer.* 64(1): 309-311.

Bhatkar A., W.H., Whitcomb, W.F. Buren, P. Callahan, and T.

Carlysle (1972). "Confrontation behavior between *Lasius neoniger* (Hymenoptera: Formicidae) and the imported fire ant." *Environ. Entomol.* 1(3): 274-279.

Callahan, P.S. and T.C. Carlysle (1972). "The scanning electron microscope in agriculture research." *Sunshine State Agric. Res. Report*, Jan-Feb., 3-6.

Goldman, L.J., P.S. Callahan, and T.C. Carlysle (1972). "Tibial combs and proboscis cleaning in mosquitoes." *Ann. Entomol. Soc. Am* 65 6): 1299-1302.

Callahan, P.S., A.N. Sparks, J.W. Snow, and W.W. Copeland (1972). "Corn earworm moth: vertical distribution in nocturnal flight." *Environ. Entomol* 1: 497-503.

Callahan, P.S. and T.C. Carlysle (1972). "Comparison of the epaulette and micronodules on the tympanic membrane of the corn earworm moth with those of the cabbage looper." *Ann. Entomol. Soc. Amer.* 65(4): 918-925.

Callahan, P. S. and H.A. Denmark (1973). "Attraction of the 'lovebug' *Plecia nearctica* (Diptera: Bibionidae) to UV irradiated automobile exhaust fumes." *Fla. Entomol.* 56(2): 113-119.

Turner, W.K. and P. S. Callahan (1973). "Electrical charge on the antenna of cabbage looper, *Trichoplusia ni* (Hubner)." *First Semi-Annual Report*, Insect Attractants, Behavior, and Basic Biology Lab., Gainesville, Fla. p. 53.

Callahan, P.S. and F. Lee (1974). "A vector analysis of the infrared emission of night flying moths, with a discussion of the system as a directional homing device." *Ann. Entomol. Soc. Am.* 67: 341-355.

Callahan, P.S. (1975). "Laser in der biologie." *Laser Elektrotoptik*, Stuttgart 2: 38-39.

Callahan, P.S. (1975). "Insect antennae with special reference to the mechanism of scent detection and the evolution of the sensilla." *Int. J. Insect Physiol. & Embryol.* 4(5): 381-430.

Callahan, P.S. (1976). "The antenna of insects as an electromagnetic sensory organ." Studies on the shootborer Hypsipyla grandella (Zeller). *Misc. Public. #101*, Vol. II. J.L. Whitmore (ed). pp. 31-41.

Callahan, P.S. (1977). "Solid state organic (pheromone-beeswax) far infrared maser." *Appl. Opt.* 16(6): 1557-1562.

Callahan, P.S. (1977). "Moth and candle: the candle flame as a sexual mimic of the coded infrared wavelengths from a moth sex scent." *Appl. Opt.* 16: 3089-3097.

Callahan, P.S. (1977). "Tapping modulation of the far infrared (17 μm region) emission from the cabbage looper pheromone (sex scent)." *Appl. Opt.* 16: 3098-3102.

Turner, W.K., P.S. Callahan, and F.L. Lee (1977). "Lack of response of cabbage looper, corn earworm and fall armyworm moths to 28, 118, and 337 μm laser radiation." *Ann. Entomol. Soc. Am.* 70(2): 234-236.

Mankin, R.W. and P.S. Callahan (1977). "Derivation of equations which relate the effective surface charge density of a dielectric or electret to measurable parameters." *J. Appl. Phys.* 48(3): 1372-1374.

Callahan, P.S. (1977). "Comments on Mark Diesendorf's critique of my review paper." *Int. J. Insect Morphol. & Embryol.* 6(2): 111-122.

Callahan, P.S. and E. Hamilton (1977). "Pumping frequency for the 17-μm ir emission from the cabbage looper moth sex scent (pheromone)." *Appl. Opt.* 16(6): 1476- 1477.

Callahan, P.S. (1977). "Tuning in to Nature." *Explorers J.* 55(4): 184-187.

Callahan, P.S. (1978). "Giant mirror of Birr." *Appl. Opt.* 17(5): 678-680.

Callahan, P.S. and R.W. Mankin (1978). "Insects as unidentified flying objects." *Appl. Opt.* 17(21): 3355-3360.

Callahan, P.S. (1979). "Insects as unidentified flying objects: author's reply to comment; 1." *Appl. Opt.* 18(16): 2724-2725.

Callahan, P. S. (1979). "Evolution of antennae, their sensilla and the mechanism of scent detection in Arthropoda." *Arthropod Phylogeny.* A.P. Gupta (ed.) Van Nostrand Reinhold Co., New York. pp. 259-298.

Callahan, P. S. (1979). "John Tyndall: unifier of 19th century science." *Appl. Opt.* 18(3): 255-258.

Callahan, P.S. (1980). 'Stimulated visible emission from insects and its relationship to nonlinear scattering of radiation and nighttime UFO sightings." *Atti della fondazione giorgio ronchi* 35: 181-190.

Callahan, P.S. (1980). "Stimulated maser-like infrared emission from water vapor doped with ammonia and insect sex attractant: biological implications." *Physiol. Chem. Phys.* 12(2): 31-38.

Mankin, R.W., K.W. Vick, M.S. Mayer, J.A. Coffelt, and P.S. Callahan (1980). "Models for dispersal of vapors in open and confined spaces: applications to sex pheromone trapping in a warehouse." *J. Chem. Ecol.* 6(5): 929-950.

Callahan, P.S. (1981). "Nonlinear IR resonance in a biological system." *Appl. Opt.* 20(22): 3827.

Callahan, P.S. (1981). "John Tyndall — contributions to the development of infrared and solid state communications." *John Tyndall, essays on a natural philosopher.* W.H. Brock, N.D. McMillan, and R.C. Mollan (eds.). Royal Dublin Society, historical studies in Irish science and technology, no. 3. pp. 129-144.

Callahan, P. S. (1982). "Narrow band IR frequency detection by insects." *Counter-measures/counter-countermeasures Center, final report.* Dept. of the Army, Washington, DC.

Callahan, P.S., J.C. Nickerson, and W.H. Whitcomb (1982). "Attraction of ants to narrow-band (maser-like) far-infrared radiation as evidence for an insect infrared communication system." *Physiol. Chem. & Physics* 14: 139-144.

Callahan, P.S. (1983). "The possible detection of magnetic monopoles and monopole tachyons." *Spec. Sci. & Technol.* 9(1): 51-60.

Callahan, P.S. (1984). "Nonlinear maserlike radiation in biological systems." *Insect Neurochemistry and Neurophysiology.* A.B. Borkovec and T.J. Kelly (eds.) Plenum Publishing Co. pp. 337-339.

Callahan, P.S. (1985). "Picket-fence interferometer on the antenna of the Noctuidae and Pyralidae moths." *Appl. Opt.* 24(14): 2217-2220.

Callahan, P.S. (1985). "Dielectric waveguide modeling at 3.0 cm of the antenna sensilla of the lovebug, *Plecia nearctica* Hardy." *Appl. Optics,* 24: 1094-1097.

Callahan, P.S., T.C. Carlysle, and H.A. Denmark (1985). "Mechanism of attraction of the lovebug, Plecia nearctica, to southern highways: further evidence for the IR-dielectric waveguide theory of insect olfaction." *Appl. Optics,* 24: 1088-1093.

Callahan, P.S. (1988). "A possible cure for AIDS — dielectric antenna theory and virion coherence." *F.D.A. Journal*

Callahan, P.S. (1989). "Treating the AIDS virus as an antenna. 21st Century." *March-April,* 26-31.

Callahan, P.S. (1989). "Maserlike nonlinear scatter from human breath, a surface-enhanced far infrared scatter effect." *Medical Hypoth.* 28: 99-105.

Callahan, P.S. (1989). "Fourier transform studies of audio stimulated surface enhanced scatter in biological systems." *High resolution fourier transform spectroscopy 1989 technical digest series.* 6: 105-108.

Callahan, P.S. (1990). "Nonlinear infrared coherent radiation as an energy coupling mechanism in living systems." *Molecular and biological physics of living systems.* R.K. Mishra (ed.)

Kluwer Academic Publishers, Netherlands. pp. 239-273.

Callahan, P.S. (1991). "Dielectric waveguide (open resonator) models of the corn earworm, sensilla: sensilla relationship to infrared coherent molecular scatter emissions from semiochemicals (Lepidoptera: Noctuidae)." *Ann. Entomol. Soc. Am.* 84(4): 361-368.

Callahan, P.S. (1993). "The mysterious round towers of Ireland: low energy radio in nature." *The Explorer's Journal,* Summer, 84-91.

Koemel, W.C. and P.S. Callahan (1994). "Relationship of extremely low frequency radio emission from flying insects to semiochemical communication." *Ann. Entomol. Soc. Am.* 87(5): 491 497.

Published Speeches:

Blum, M. S. and P.S. Callahan (1960). "Chemical and biological properties of the venom of the imported fire ant (*Solenopsis saevissima v.* Richter Forel) and the isolation of the insecticidal component." *Proc. XI Inter. Cong. Ent. Vienna, Austria.* pp. 290-293.

Callahan, P.S. (1960). "A morphological study of spermatophore placement and mating in the subfamily Plusiinae (Noctuidae: Lepidoptera)." *Proc. XI Inter. Congr. Ent. Vienna, Austria.* pp. 339-345.

Callahan, P.S. (1964). 'A photographic analysis of moth flight behavior with special reference to the theory for electromagnetic radiation as an attractive force between the sexes and to host plants." *Proc. XII Inter. Congr. Ent. London, England.* p. 302.

Callahan, P.S. (1965). "Electromagnetic communication in insects . . . determination of infrared radiance, emissivity, and temperature of arthropods." *Digest 6th Inter. Conf. Med. Electr. Biol. Engin. 34-5 Toyko, Japan.* pp. 583-584.

Callahan, P.S. (1965). "Are arthropods infrared and microwave detectors?" *Proc. N. Cen. Br. ESA* 20: 20-31.

Callahan, P.S. (1965). "Electromagnetic communication in insects . . . elements of the terrestrial infrared environment: including generation, transmission, and detection by moths." *Sci. AAAS Symposium, Montreal, Canada.*

Callahan, P.S. (1966). "Electronic instrumentation for infrared and microwave studies of insect communication systems." Proc. 19th Ann. Conf. Eng. Med. & Biol. 22: 157.

Callahan, P.S. (1967). "Electronic instrumentation for studying the insect communication system." *Proc. N. Cen. Br. ESA* 22: 28-36.

Chapin, J.B. and P.S. Callahan (1967). "A list of the Noctuidae (Lepidoptera, Insecta) collected in the vicinity of Baton Rouge, Louisiana." *Proc. La. Acad. Sc. XXX* pp. 3948.

Callahan, P.S. (1969). "The radiation environment and its relationship to possible methods of environmental control of insects." *Proc. Tall Timbers Conf. Ecol. Anim. Contr. Hab. Manag.* February 27-28, 1969. pp. 85-108.

Callahan, P.S. (1969). "Insect communication: the antenna as an electromagnetic sensory organ. Proc. Symp. on Potentials In Crop Protection." *N.Y. Agric. Exp. Stn., Geneva, N.Y.* May 20-21, 1969. pp. 3945.

Callahan, P.S. (1970). "Insects and the radiation environment." *Proc. Tall Timbers Conf. Ecol. Anim. Contr. Hab. Manag.* February 26-28, 1970. pp. 247-258.

Callahan, P.S. (1970). "Insect bioelectronics: a theoretical and experimental study of the dielectric properties of insect sensors." *Proc. Feder. Automatic Contr., Symp. Biol. Aspects Contr. Cybernetics. Yenevan, U.S.S.R.*, Vol. 1, pp. 48-63. (in Russian).

Callahan, P.S. (1970). "Sensory reception in insects." *Proc. 5th Forest Insect and Disease Contr. Conf., S.U. Forest Service, Atlanta, Ga.*, pp. 57-77.

Callahan, P.S. (1971). "Insects and the unsensed environment." *Proc. Tall Timbers Conf. Ecol. Anim. Contr. Hab. Manag.* February 25-27, 1971. pp. 85-96.

Callahan, P.S. and H.A. Denmark (1973). "The 'lovebug' phenomenon." *Proc. Tall Timbers Conf. Ecol. Anim. Contr. by Habitat Manag.* 5: 93-101.

Callahan, P. S. (1973). "Studies on the shoot-borer *Hypsipyla grandella* (Zellar) (Lep., Pyralidae). XIX. The antenna of insects as an electromagnetic sensory organ." *Proc. Symp. Contr. of Hypsipyla. Turrialba* 23(3): 263-274.

Callahan, P.S. (1975). "The insect antenna as a dielectric array for the detection of infrared radiation from molecules." *1st Internat. Conf. Biomed. Transducers, Paris, France.* pp. 133-138.

Callahan, P.S. (1978). "Nonlinear radiation and life — the human breath as a low intensity gasdynamic laser." *Proc. Internat. Conf. Lasers.* December 11-15, 1978. pp. 99-103.

Callahan, P.S. (1979). "Night glowing phenomenon as an indicator of insect migration routes." *Movement of Highly Mobile Insects: concepts and methodology in research.* R.L. Rabb and G.G. Kennedy (eds.) Chap. 18. pp. 257-262. *Proc. Conf. Movement of selected species of Lepidoptera in the Southeastern United States, Raleigh, NC.* Apr. 9-11, 1979.

Callahan, P.S. (1981). "Non-linear infrared radiation in biological systems with special reference to future medical applications." *Proc. 4th Inter. Conf. Human Functioning. Garvey*

Center, Witchita, Kansas. September 12-14, 1980. pp. 137- 156.

Callahan, P.S. (1982). "Low energy electromagnetic radiation in relationship to body functions." *Proc. 5th Inter. Conf. Human Functioning. Garvey Center, Witchita, Kansas.* September 17-20, 1981. pp. 159-172.

Callahan, P.S. (1983). "The possible detection of magnetic monopoles and monopole tachyons." *Proc. 2nd Inter. Symp. Nonconventional Energy Technol. Atlanta, Georgia.* September 9-11, 1983. pp. 87-98.

Callahan, P.S. (1985). "New discoveries in the maser-like control frequencies of life." *Proc. 9th Inter. Conf. Human Functioning. Garvey Center, Wichita, Kansas.* September 1 3- 15, 1985.

Callahan, P.S. (1988). "Maserlike nonlinear scatter from human breath — cabannes far infrared scatter effect and its relation to the AIDS virus." *Proc. Inter. Conf. Nonlinear Opt.* pp. 57-61.

Callahan, P.S. (1989). "Fourier transform studies of audio stimulated surface enhanced scatter in biological systems (insects)." *High Resolution Fourier Transform Spectroscopy, Topical Meeting. Proc. Opt. Soc. Am., Santa Fe, New Mexico.* February 13-15, 1989.

Callahan, P.S. (1990). "Solar energy — the nature of natural and 'EWEC' solar collections." *Proc 3rd Inter. New Energy Symp. Hull Quebec, Canada.* pp. 139-145.

Callahan, P.S. (1992). "Photonic ionic radio amplifier for pumping IR radiation from living systems." *Proc. Opt. Soc. Am Albuquerque, New Mexico.* Sept. 20-25, 1992.

Monographs:

'The exoskeleton of the corn earworm moth, *Heliothis zea* Lepidoptera: Noctuidae with special reference to the sensilla as polytubular dielectric arrays (1969)." *Univ. Ga. Clg. Agric. Exper. Stat. Res. Bull.* 54. 105 pp.

Callahan, P.S. (1981) "The Tilma: under infra-red radiation." *CARA studies on popular devotion*, Wash. D.C. Vol II: Guadalupan studies, No. 3. 45 pp.

Books:

Insect Behavior. (1971) Four Winds Press, New York. 155 pp.

Insects and How They Function. (1971) Holiday House, New York. 191 pp.

The Evolution of Insects. (1972) Holiday House, New York. 192 pp.

The Magnificent Birds of Prey. (1974) Holiday House, New York. 190 pp.

Bird Behavior. (1975) Four Winds Press, New York. 188 pp.

Tuning Into Nature. (1975) Devin-Adair, Old Greenwich, Conn. 240 pp. (translated into Japanese).

Birds and How They Function. (1979) Holiday House, New York. 156 pp.

The Soul of the Ghost Moth. (1981) Devin-Adair, Old Greenwich, Conn. 108 pp.

Ancient Mysteries Modern Visions. (1984) Acres U.S.A., Metairie, Louisiana. 142 pp.

A Walk in the Sun. (1988) Acres U.S.A., Metairie, Louisiana. 241 pp.

Nature's Silent Music (1992) Acres U.S.A., Metairie, Louisiana. 224 pp.

Exploring the Spectrum (1994) Acres U.S.A., Metairie, Louisiana. 178 pp.

Paramagnetism (1996) Acres U.S.A., Metairie, Louisiana. 128 pp.

Research featured in: (partial listing)

Electronics (1965). "Bioengineering: a new discipline." 38(12): 111 -118.

Agricultural Research (1966). "Do moths use radar?"14(8): 3-4.

Time (1968). "Lifesaving light." 92(9): 48.

NASA Activities (1975). "Nature provides clues for solar energy conversion." 6(5): 9.

The Furrow (1978). "Getting along with Nature and Visionaries of 'Agri-Biology.' September-October: 4-5.

Time (1978) Pesky UFOs. l 12(21): 81.

Index